Letts GCSE Success

Revision Guide

Edexcel Science Foundation

Brian Arnold • Hannah Kingston • Emma Poole

Contents

Biology

Chemistry

Physics

Pyramids

A *food chain* shows us simply who eats who: a *food web* is a series of linked food chains and provides a more realistic picture. *Energy* enters the food chain when plants absorb sunlight during photosynthesis. The Sun's energy supports all life on earth.

Pyramids of numbers

A **pyramid of numbers** tells us the **number** of organisms involved at each stage in a food chain. At each level of the food chain (**trophic level**) the number of organisms generally reduces.

| fox |
| rabbit |
| grass |

Sometimes a pyramid of numbers doesn't look like a pyramid at all as it doesn't take into account the size of the organisms.

blackbird		fleas
ladybirds		fox
aphids		rabbits
rose bush		lettuce

A rose bush counts as one organism, but a rose bush can support many herbivores. In this pyramid of numbers, the top carnivores are fleas that feed on a single fox.

Pyramids of biomass

A **pyramid of biomass** takes into account the **mass of an organism** at each level. If we take the information from the pyramid of numbers and multiply it by the mass of the organisms, we get a pyramid shape again.

A single rose bush weighs more than the many aphids feeding on it, and the aphids weigh more than the few ladybirds that feed

| blackbird |
| ladybirds |
| aphids |
| rose bush |

on them. Finally, a blackbird weighs less than the many ladybirds it feeds on.

Loss of energy in food chains 1

Food chains rarely have more than four or five links. This is because they lose energy along the way: the final organism is only receiving a fraction of the energy that was produced at the beginning of the chain.

Plants absorb their energy from the Sun. Only a fraction of this energy is converted into glucose during photosynthesis. Some energy is lost to decomposers as the plant sheds leaves, seeds or fruit. The plant also uses energy during growth and reproduction.

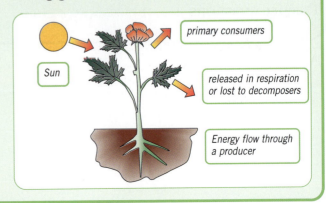

Sun

primary consumers

released in respiration or lost to decomposers

Energy flow through a producer

Loss of energy in food chains 2

It is the increase in biomass achieved through this growth that provides food for herbivores. However, only approximately 10% of the original energy from the Sun is passed on to the primary consumer through the plant's biomass. The primary consumer also experiences energy losses and only 10% of their total energy intake is passed on to the secondary consumer.

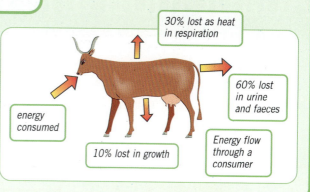

30% lost as heat in respiration

60% lost in urine and faeces

energy consumed

10% lost in growth

Energy flow through a consumer

Where does the energy go?

The 90% energy loss at each stage is spent on life processes such as **respiration**. Respiration **releases heat energy** into the surroundings. Animals that are warm-blooded use up energy **keeping warm** and a great deal of energy is also lost through **urine and faeces. In addition, not all of the organism's body mass is eaten.**

 A common exam question is about the energy losses in food chains and how to reduce them. Make sure that you learn them thoroughly.

Efficiency of food production

We must look at ways of improving the **efficiency** of food production and reducing losses. There are two ways this can be done:

1 Reduce the number of stages in the food chain. It is more energy efficient to eat plant produce than meat.
2 Rear animals intensively – if their movement is restricted, we use antibiotics to keep disease at bay and they are kept warm, they will not require as much food. Less energy will be lost in life processes.

There is always competition for resources in a food web. Try to imagine the effect a change in one organism's numbers will have on the rest of the food web.

QUICK TEST

1 Why do food chains only have four or five links?

2 What do pyramids of numbers show?

3 What don't pyramids of numbers take into account?

4 What pyramids can be drawn using the mass of animals and plants?

5 From where does a plant get its original energy source?

6 Approximately how much energy is passed on from the producer to the consumer?

7 Why do warm-blooded animals need to eat a lot of food?

8 In animals, where does most of the energy go?

9 List the ways that energy is lost in food chains.

10 How can we reduce energy losses in food chains?

Adaptation and competition

A habitat is where an *organism* lives: it provides the conditions needed for that organism to survive. A community consists of living things in the habitat. Each community is made up of different populations of animals and plants. Each population is adapted to live in that particular habitat. An ecosystem is made up of all living things and their physical environment.

Sizes of populations

Populations cannot keep growing until numbers are out of control. The issues that affect the size of the population and prevent it from becoming too large are called **limiting factors**. They are:

- the amount of food and water available
- the predators and grazing – who may eat the animal or plant

- disease
- climate – temperature, floods, droughts and storms
- **competition** – for space, mates, light, food and water
- human activity – such as pollution or destruction of habitats.

Adaptation

A polar bear lives in the cold, Arctic regions of the world. It has many features that enable it to survive:

- It has a **thick coat** to keep in body heat, as well as a layer of blubber for insulation.
- Its coat is white and blends into its surroundings.
- Its fur is greasy and so does not hold water after swimming. This prevents any cooling by evaporation.
- A polar bear has **big feet** to spread its weight on snow and ice. It also has big sharp claws to catch fish.
- It is a **good swimmer** and **runner** in order to catch prey.
- The shape of a polar bear is **compact** even though it is large. This keeps its surface area to a minimum to reduce loss of body heat.

A camel has features that enable it to survive in the hot deserts of the world:

- The camel has an ability to **drink** a lot of water and **store** it.
- It loses very little water as it produces **little urine** and can cope with big changes in temperature so there is no need for sweating.
- All its fat is stored in the humps so there is **no insulating layer** of fat.
- Its sandy colour provides **camouflage**.
- It has a **large surface area** to enable it to lose heat.

The adaptations of a camel and polar bear are two popular examples. Be aware that other animals and plants, such as the cactus, have also adapted to live in their environments.

Competition

Growing **populations** may result in overcrowding and limited resources to support increased numbers.

Animals have to compete for **space, food and water** in their struggle to stay alive. Only the strongest and best adapted will survive, leading to the process of survival of the fittest.

Plants compete for **space, light, water and nutrients**. The weed is a very successful competitor: look at the diagram on the right to see how.

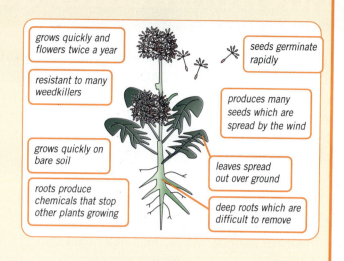

grows quickly and flowers twice a year

seeds germinate rapidly

resistant to many weedkillers

produces many seeds which are spread by the wind

grows quickly on bare soil

leaves spread out over ground

roots produce chemicals that stop other plants growing

deep roots which are difficult to remove

Predator/prey graphs

In a community, the number of animals stays fairly constant. This is partly due to the amount of food limiting the size of the populations. A **predator** is an animal that hunts and kills another animal. The **prey** is the hunted animal. As you can see, predator and prey population levels go in cycles.

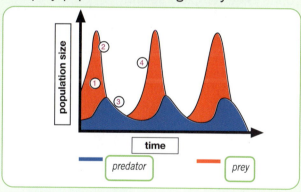

1 If the population of prey increases, there is more food for the predator, so its numbers increase.
2 This causes the number of prey to decrease as they are eaten.
3 This, in turn, causes the number of predators to decrease, as there is not enough food to support the increased numbers of predators and they must compete with one another for food.
4 If the predator numbers fall, the prey numbers can increase again, as they are no longer being eaten, and so on.

KEY TERMS

Make sure you understand these terms before moving on!

- organisms
- populations
- limiting factors
- competition
- adaptation
- predator/prey graph

QUICK TEST

1 What is a habitat?
2 What makes up a community?
3 What makes up a population?
4 What things do plants compete for?
5 How does the polar bear's coat help it survive in the Arctic?
6 What factor determines whether animals or plants survive in their environments?

Environmental damage

Improvements in agriculture, health and medicine have led to a dramatic rise in the human population. An increase in population size leads to an increase in pollution and more demands on the world's resources.

Intensive farming

Farming has had to become more intensive to provide more food from a given area of land. Intensive farming can produce more food but it has problems. Many people regard intensive farming of animals as cruel. In order to produce more food from the land, fertilisers and pesticides are needed.

Pesticides

Pesticides are used to kill insects that damage crops. They also kill harmless insects, which can cause a shortage of food for insect-eating birds. There is always the danger that pesticides will be washed into rivers and lakes and **end up in our food chains**. This was the case in the 1960s when a pesticide called DDT got into the food chain and threatened populations of animals.

Fertilisers

Plants need minerals, which they take up from the soil, to grow. During intensive-farming methods, nutrients are used up quickly, and the farmer is forced to replace them with artificial fertilisers. Fertilisers enable farmers to produce more crops in a smaller area of land and can reduce the need to destroy the countryside for extra space.

Destruction of the land and seas

An increase in industry has led to the need to take over the land, which destroys wildlife and causes pollution.

we use land for building

...dumping our rubbish

...getting raw materials

...farming to feed the world

Deforestation

In the UK there are already few forests left. In other, under-developed countries they are **chopping down forests** (called deforestation) to provide timber or space for agriculture. This causes several problems for the environment. Burning this timber increases the level of carbon dioxide in the air. Forests absorb carbon dioxide in the air and provide us with oxygen. Deforestation leads to soil erosion as the soil is exposed to rain and wind. The trees evaporate water into the air and without it there will be a decrease in rainfall. Destroying forests also destroys many different animal and plant habitats.

What can be done?

The problems will get worse unless people can learn to limit their needs. A possible solution to some of the problems is **organic farming**. Organic farming uses **manure as a fertiliser** and **sets aside land** to allow wild plants and animals to flourish. It relies on the **biological control of pests**, i.e. the use of other animals to eat pests. It is not so effective but produces no harmful effects.

We can also look at developing **alternative energy sources** such as solar power and wind energy. This will help conserve the world's rapidly diminishing fossil fuel supply.

> *Learn the arguments for and against intensive farming. Look at the benefits of its alternative, organic farming.*

Conservation and sustainable development

With the human population increasing and using up resources, we need to find a way of keeping the quality of life for future generations. This is known as **sustainable development**.

It is important to protect our food supply, maintain biodiversity, prevent animals and plants from becoming extinct and conserve resources as we do not know what the future may hold.

KEY TERMS

Make sure you understand these terms before moving on!
- intensive farming
- fertilisers
- pesticides
- deforestation
- organic farming
- sustainable development

QUICK TEST

1. Why has the human population increased in last few hundred years?

2. What problems can the use of pesticides cause?

3. What is the alternative to pesticides?

4. Name four ways that humans reduce the amount of land.

5. What is deforestation?

6. How does deforestation contribute to the greenhouse effect?

7. What other problems does deforestation cause?

8. What could be used as an alternative to fertilisers?

9. Name ways in which we can reduce harmful effects on the environment.

10. Why are organic products more expensive than non-organic products?

Evolution

Evolution is all about gradual change and improvement from simple life forms. The theory of evolution states that all living things that exist today, or once existed, evolved from simple life forms three billion years ago. *Natural selection* is the process that causes evolution.

The theory of evolution

Religious theories are based on the need for a 'creator' for all life to exist on Earth, but there are other theories. **Charles Darwin**, a British naturalist, first put forward his theory about 140 years ago. Darwin visited the Galapagos Islands off the coast of South America and made a number of observations that led to his theory of evolution:

- Organisms produce more offspring than could possibly survive.
- Population numbers remain fairly constant despite this.
- All organisms in a species show variation.

- Some of these variations are inherited.

He also concluded from these observations that, since more offspring were produced than could survive, there must be a struggle for existence. It was this struggle for existence that led to the strongest and fittest offspring surviving and passing genes on to their offspring. This is sometimes called the **'survival of the fittest' or natural selection.**

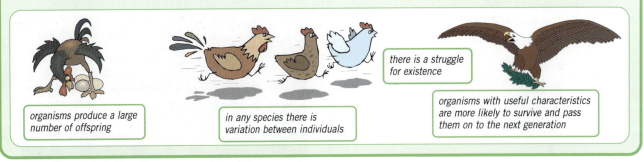

organisms produce a large number of offspring

in any species there is variation between individuals

there is a struggle for existence

organisms with useful characteristics are more likely to survive and pass them on to the next generation

Other theories

- In the seventeenth century, an archbishop called James Usher declared that God created all life forms, from the very simple to the most complex. He dated the beginning of all life from Monday, 3rd October 4004 BC.
- In the eighteenth century the Conte de Buffon, a French zoologist, proposed that living things changed over time due to the environment or chance. He also proposed that humans and apes were related.

- Erasmus Darwin (father to Charles) believed in evolution but did not know what caused it.
- More ideas followed that came closer to Darwin's theory. Some thought that natural disasters and changes to the Earth had shaped organisms, killing off species that were unable to adapt and allowing new life forms to develop. Scientists also began looking at fossil evidence.

Natural selection

Darwin stated that the process of natural selection was the basis for evolution. A **species** is defined as a group of living things able to breed together and produce fertile offspring. Within a species there is variation between individuals. Changes in the environment may affect some individuals and not others.

Only those who can adapt to suit their new environment survive to breed and pass on their advantageous genes. The factors that prevent all offspring surviving are competition for food, predators and disease. Eventually, nature decides which individuals should breed. There is a 'survival of the fittest'.

Scientific concept

Despite some strong opposition, Darwin's theory stood the test of time and became widely accepted. A man called **Lamarck** suggested another theory, that animals evolved features according to how much they used them. Giraffes, for example, grew longer necks because they needed to reach food.

In practice, the combined effects of natural selection, selective breeding, genetic engineering and mutation may lead to a new species forming. All these processes are still taking place and so evolution is still occurring.

KEY TERMS

Make sure you understand these terms before moving on!
- evolution
- natural selection
- Charles Darwin
- species
- Lamarck

QUICK TEST

1. When did life forms first exist?
2. Whose theory of evolution was gradually accepted?
3. What prevents all the organisms in a species surviving?
4. Which individuals would survive a change in the environment?
5. What process causes evolution?
6. Where did Darwin make the observations that led to his theory?
7. Define the word 'species'.
8. What was Darwin's observation when he looked at the individuals in a species?
9. Why was there a struggle for existence within a population?
10. Does evolution happen gradually or occur suddenly?

Evidence for evolution

Fossils

Fossils are the remains of dead organisms that lived millions of years ago found in rocks. Most dead organisms decay and disintegrate. Fossils can be formed in the following ways:

- The hard parts of animals that do not decay form into a rock.
- Minerals, which preserve their shape, gradually replace the softer parts of animals that decay very slowly.
- The conditions needed for the decay of dead animals and plants are oxygen, moisture and warmth. When one or more of these conditions are absent, then fossils of the remains may form.

Fossils provide **evidence** for evolution preserved in rock. The younger fossils are generally found nearer the surface of the rock.

The evolution of the horse is clearly illustrated by fossils. Natural selection has operated to produce the modern horse.

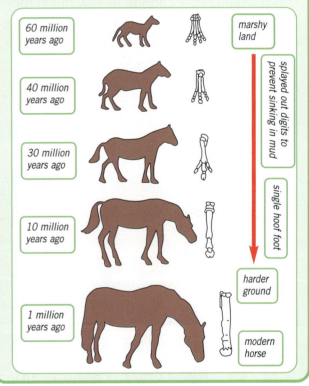

60 million years ago		marshy land
40 million years ago		splayed out digits to prevent sinking in mud
30 million years ago		
10 million years ago		single hoof foot
1 million years ago		harder ground
		modern horse

Natural selection in action

An example of the environment causing changes in a species is that of the **peppered moth**. The moth lives in woodlands on lichen-covered trees. There are two types of peppered moth: a light, speckled form and a dark form. The dark-coloured moth was the result of a mutation and was usually eaten by predators.

| dark-coloured moth against a soot-covered tree | the pale moth is at a disadvantage in polluted areas |

In the 1850s, the dark moth was rare. As pollution from factories began to blacken tree trunks, the dark moth was at an advantage because it was camouflaged. In 1895, most of the population of moths were dark. In cleaner, less polluted areas, the light moth had an advantage against predators and so it still survived to breed.

> 💡 *The peppered moth and the evolution of the horse are popular examples used to demonstrate evolution by natural selection.*

Mutations

Mutations that occur in genes are usually harmful. In the case of the peppered moth, mutation turned out to be useful when the environment changed. Over a long period of time, gradual changes (mutations) may result in totally new species being formed. This brings us back to the theory of evolution that all species evolved from a common ancestor that existed billions of years ago.

Extinction

Species that are unable to adapt to their surroundings become extinct. Examples include the mammoth, the dodo and the sabre-toothed tiger. **Extinction** can also be caused by changes in the environment, new predators, new disease, new competition or human activity such as hunting, pollution or destruction of habitat.

mammoth | dodo | sabre-toothed tiger

Classification

Classification is a way of sorting living things into groups according to their similarities and differences. Carl Linnaeus devised a classification system based on features including body shape, types of limbs and skeleton. The smallest group of living things is called a **species** and the largest is called a kingdom. There are five kingdoms including animals and plants. As you move down the classification system, the animals or plants have more and more in common until they can only belong to the same species. For example, humans and apes belong in the same animal kingdom but are different species. Species contain animals or plants that have several features in common but also show variation, as in different breeds of dog. Different species can still be very similar and live in similar types of habitat. This can make classification difficult.

An example is that of the Galapagos finch considered by Charles Darwin. He studied many different varieties of finches and concluded that they shared a common ancestor but had evolved into different species because they had lived in and adapted to different habitats by flying to various islands around the mainland.

KEY TERMS

Make sure you understand these terms before moving on!

- fossils
- evidence
- natural selection in action
- peppered moth
- mutations
- extinction
- classification
- species

QUICK TEST

1. Why did the feet of the modern horse change?

2. Which type of peppered moth would survive in industrial regions and why?

3. What conditions must be absent for fossils to form?

4. What is the prime reason that organisms become extinct?

5. What are fossils?

6. Is it possible for fossils to form in the Arctic?

7. What caused the light-coloured peppered moth to change colour?

8. How could humans cause a species to become extinct?

9. Where are young fossils found in relation to older fossils?

10. What process has produced the modern-day horse?

Selective breeding

Selective breeding involves humans breeding in the features that we want in a plant or animal, and breeding out features that we don't want. As it is humans who do the selecting rather than nature, we call this process *artificial selection.*

Artificial selection

People are always trying to breed animals and plants with special characteristics, for example a fast racehorse or a cow that produces lots of milk. Breeding must be carried out within the same species: different species cannot breed together.

The procedures involved in artificial selection are:

- Select the individuals with the best characteristics.
- Breed them together using sexual reproduction.
- Some of the offspring will, hopefully, have inherited the desirable features. The best offspring are selected and are bred together.
- This process is repeated over generations until the offspring have all the desired characteristics.

It is impossible to breed a racehorse that will win every race using sexual reproduction as there is always a variation in the offspring, and the environment the offspring is reared in will also play its part. We just have to hope that breeding two successful horses together will produce successful foals.

large but tasteless

If these two strawberry plants were selectively bred then a large *and* tasty strawberry may occur

tasty but small

Selective breeding in plants

Sexual reproduction always produces variation. With plants, variation can be overcome by producing clones, which are genetically identical individuals. To produce clones, reproduction must be asexual. Many plants reproduce asexually on their own, such as strawberry plants which produce runners, potatoes, onions and *chlorophytum* (spider plants).

Selective breeding in animals

Cows have been selectively bred to produce superior quality milk. Beef cattle have been bred to produce better meat. Dogs have been selectively bred over many years to produce the variety of breeds that we have today. Dogs, however different they may appear from poodle to Great Dane, all belong to the same species and are descended from the wolf.

Tissue culture

Gardeners can produce identical, new plants by taking **cuttings** from the original, parent plant. The plants are dipped in a rooting powder that contains hormones and kept in a damp atmosphere in order to grow into new plants. The new plants are **clones**.

Tissue culture is a technique used by commercial plant breeders. They take just a few plant cells and grow a new plant from them, using a special growth medium containing hormones. The advantages of this method are that new plants with special properties, such as resistance to diseases, can be grown quickly and cheaply all year round.

Plants also produce sexually, attracting insects for pollination. The resulting plants show variation. This is very important as if all plants only produced clones, a new disease could kill the entire species.

Problems with selective breeding

Continued breeding of closely related animals is now common, particularly for showing purposes.

This can lead to problems with infertility and reduced resistance to disease, as well as other health problems. If animals or plants are continually bred from the same, best animals or plants, all animals and plants will become very similar. This could leave the new animals and plants unable to cope with a change in the environment, and no alleles left to selectively breed new varieties of plants and animals. It is, therefore, vital to keep wild varieties alive, just in case.

 Make sure that you can list the advantages and disadvantages of the methods of selective breeding.

KEY TERMS

Make sure you understand these terms before moving on!
- selective breeding
- artificial selection
- cuttings
- clones
- tissue culture

QUICK TEST

1. What is 'selective breeding'?
2. What is the difference between artificial selection and natural selection?
3. What are 'clones'?
4. Race-winning horses are often put to stud, with people paying thousands of pounds to have them mate with their female horses. Explain why.
5. Name two methods of selective breeding in plants.
6. What is the main disadvantage of selective breeding?
7. When a gardener takes cuttings, is he using sexual reproduction or asexual reproduction to grow new plants?
8. Why should you not breed from two closely related animals such as dogs?
9. What type of reproduction produces clones?

Genes and chromosomes

Chromosomes

Inside nearly all cells is a **nucleus**. The nucleus contains instructions that control all your characteristics. The code's instructions are carried on **chromosomes**. On the chromosome there are **genes** that control each particular characteristic. Different genes control the development of different characteristics.

Inside human cells there are 46 chromosomes or 23 pairs of chromosomes. The cell is called a diploid cell. Other animals have different numbers of chromosomes.

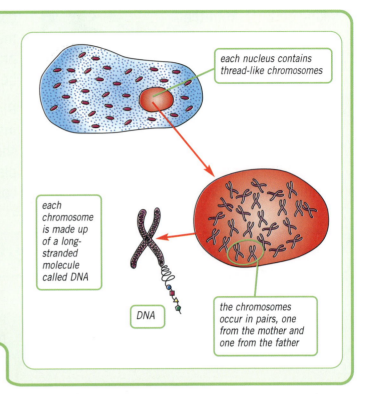

each nucleus contains thread-like chromosomes

each chromosome is made up of a long-stranded molecule called DNA

DNA

the chromosomes occur in pairs, one from the mother and one from the father

Genes and alleles

Each nucleus contains thread-like chromosomes. The chromosomes occur in pairs, one from the mother and one from the father. Each chromosome is made up of a long-stranded molecule called **DNA**. A gene is a section of DNA. Proteins and enzymes control all our characteristics: genes are chemical instructions that code for a particular protein or enzyme and, therefore, characteristic. We call the different versions of a gene **alleles**. Alleles pass on characteristics from each parent: some alleles pass on diseases. Cystic fibrosis is caused by a recessive allele. Both parents must have the cystic fibrosis allele for the disease to be inherited. Huntington's chorea is caused by a dominant allele. Only one parent needs to have the allele for the disease to be inherited.

Inheritance

To inherit characteristics from a parent's DNA, some form of reproduction needs to take place. There are two forms of reproduction:

- **Asexual reproduction** involves only one parent. The offspring have exact copies of the parental genes. There is no fusing (joining) of the parental **gametes** (sperm and eggs). Asexual reproduction produces clones: there is no variation.
- **Sexual reproduction** involves fertilisation and two parents. The gametes' nuclei fuse and the genes are passed on to the offspring. The offspring are not genetically identical. Sexual reproduction leads to variation, not only between different species of plants and animals but also between individuals of the same species.

Differences are partly due to the **inheritance** of genes from the parents but also the **environment** in which the offspring live and grow.

DNA molecule

The 'arms' of a chromosome are made up of a coiled up DNA molecule. The DNA molecule is joined together by chemical bases, like the rungs in a ladder. The two rungs of the ladder are coiled together to form a double helix.
DNA has the ability to copy itself exactly so that any new cells made have exactly the same genetic information.

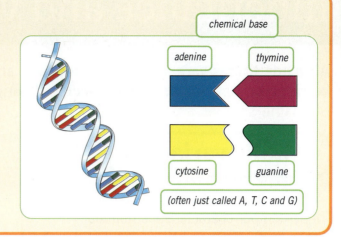

chemical base

adenine thymine

cytosine guanine

(often just called A, T, C and G)

Mutations

DNA is a very stable molecule. Occasionally, however, things can go wrong in the copying process.

KEY TERMS

Make sure you understand these terms before moving on!

- nucleus
- chromosomes
- genes
- DNA
- alleles
- asexual reproduction
- gametes
- sexual reproduction

A mutation is a change in the chemical structure of a gene or chromosome that alters the way in which an organism develops. The change may happen for no reason, or there may be a definite cause. Mutations occur naturally in the environment, for example new strains of the flu virus are always appearing. Mutations that occur in the cells of the body are not inherited: they are only harmful to the person whose body cells are altered. Mutations that occur in reproductive cells are inherited. The child will develop abnormally or die at an early age. Some inherited mutations are beneficial and form the basis of evolution.

💡 *There are lots of new, key words on this page. Make sure that you learn their definitions.*

QUICK TEST

1. What are the thread-like features contained in the nucleus called?

2. What actually controls all our characteristics?

3. What are genes?

4. Where are genes found?

5. In what circumstances are mutations inherited?

6. How many chromosomes does a human body cell have and where are they found?

7. How many genes are there for each feature?

8. What are the human gametes?

9. Which type of reproduction formed you? What else has an effect on how you look and behave?

Inheritance and variation

All living things vary in the way they look and behave. *Variation* can be between species or within species. Living things that belong to the same species are all slightly different.

Genetic variation

We look like we do because we have inherited our characteristics from our parents. Brothers and sisters are not exactly the same as each other because they inherit different genes from their parents and this process is completely random. There are thousands of different genes in every human cell, and so the combination of genes in a cell is endless. The chance of two people having the same genes is virtually impossible. The exception is identical twins who possess identical genes.

Environmental variation

The 'environment' is your surroundings and all the things that may affect your upbringing. For example, identical twins who were separated at birth and grew up in totally different surroundings following different diets could grow up looking dissimilar. The differences between the twins would be due to the environment they were brought up in, as they have identical genes. Many of the differences between people are caused by a combination of genetic and environmental influences.

Variation in plants

Plants are more affected than animals by small changes in the environment. Sunlight, temperature, moisture level and mineral levels in the soil will all determine how well a plant grows. A plant cultivated in sunlight will grow much faster and may reach double the size of a plant grown in the shade. However, a dog living in England would show no significant changes if it moved to Africa.

Variation in animals

We vary because of the random way our genes are inherited. The environment can affect most of our characteristics and it is usually a combination of the two that determines how we look and behave. Just how significant the environment is in determining our features is difficult to assess. For example, is being good at sport inherited or is it due to your upbringing?

There are some characteristics that are not affected by the environment at all. They are:

1 eye colour
2 natural hair colour
3 blood group
4 inherited diseases.

Genetics 1

Genetics is the study of how information is passed on from generation to generation. Genetic diagrams are used to show how certain characteristics are passed on.

Definitions
■ A gene is the unit of inheritance carried on **chromosomes**.

■ Alternative forms of a gene are called **alleles**.
■ **Recessive** refers to the weaker allele.
■ **Dominant** refers to the stronger allele.

Genetics 2

- The **genotype** is the type of alleles an organism carries.
- The **phenotype** is what the organism physically looks like, the result of what genotype the organism has.

- When an organism has different alleles they are said to be **heterozygous** but if they have the same alleles in their genotype then they are **homozygous**.

A worked example – inheritance of eye colour

Letters are used to represent alleles, typically upper case for dominant characteristics and lower case for recessive characteristics. Remember, we have two alleles for eye colour, one from each parent, making up a gene.

- The allele for brown eyes is dominant and so can be represented by the letter B.
- The allele for blue eyes is recessive so that is represented by the letter b.

- If the mother and father are both heterozygous for eye colour, they will have the genotype Bb.

What colour eyes will their children have?

We can show the possible outcomes using a Punnett square:

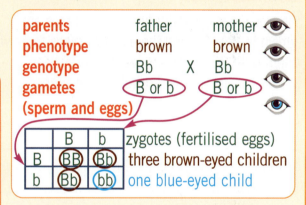

parents	father	mother	
phenotype	brown	brown	
genotype	Bb	X	Bb	
gametes (sperm and eggs)	B or b	B or b	

	B	b	zygotes (fertilised eggs)
B	BB	Bb	three brown-eyed children
b	Bb	bb	one blue-eyed child

This gives a 3 : 1 ratio of brown to blue eyes.

💡 *Try to learn all the definitions on these pages.*

KEY TERMS

Make sure you understand these terms before moving on!

- variation
- environment
- inherited
- genetics
- recessive
- dominant

QUICK TEST

1. What do we use to represent alleles in genetic diagrams?

2. Why are brothers or sisters not identical?

3. What does 'recessive' mean?

4. What does 'dominant' mean?

5. What four environmental factors determine the growth of plants?

6. Why do animals and plants of the same species vary?

7. Are identical twins always identical? If not, why not?

8. How can we show possible outcomes of a genetic cross?

9. What are alleles?

10. Which of the following characteristics is definitely inherited: blood group, hair colour, spoken language?

Genetic engineering

Genetic engineering is the process by which genes from one organism are removed and inserted into the cells of another.

Gene therapy

It may be possible to use genetic engineering to treat inherited diseases such as cystic fibrosis. Sufferers could be cured if the correct gene could be inserted into their body cells. The problem that exists with cystic fibrosis is that the cells that need the correct gene are found in many parts of the body, which makes it difficult to remove them to insert the required gene. Even if the correct gene was inserted into the body cells, the cells would not multiply. As a result, there would be many cells that still have the faulty gene.

GM crops

At present, no genetically modified crops are grown in the UK, and there are no plans to grow them until 2008. They have, however, been grown for research and development purposes.

Countries that do grow GM crops include the USA, Argentina, Canada and China. What they grow, and in what quantities, varies from country to country but the crops often include corn, cotton and soybean.

The benefits of genetic engineering

Genetic engineering benefits industry, medicine and agriculture in many ways. We have developed plants that are resistant to pests and diseases, and plants that can grow in less desirable conditions. Wheat and other crops have been developed that can take nitrogen directly from the air and produce proteins without the need for costly fertilisers. Tomatoes and other sorts of fruit are now able to stay fresh for longer.

Tomatoes can be genetically engineered to stay fresh for longer by inserting a gene from fish into their cells. Would you eat one?

Risks of genetic engineering

Manipulating bacteria for use in producing proteins could result in previously harmless bacteria mutating into disease-causing bacteria. There is also concern about potential damage to human health, whether GM crops cause allergies and the notion of eating 'foreign' DNA. Will the nutritional quality of the food remain the same? Will the environment suffer when crops cross pollinate with weeds so that the gene that breeds resistance to disease is transferred to the weeds and they become resistant to herbicides and pesticides? There is a possibility that human eggs can be taken out of the womb and the harmful genes removed before the egg is inserted back into the womb to continue its growth. Genetic engineering is seen by many as manipulating the 'stuff of life'. Is it morally and ethically wrong to interfere with nature?

Manipulating genes

Genetic engineering has been used to treat diabetic people through the production of the protein, insulin.

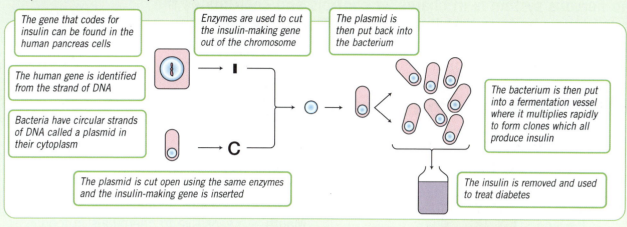

The gene that codes for insulin can be found in the human pancreas cells

The human gene is identified from the strand of DNA

Bacteria have circular strands of DNA called a plasmid in their cytoplasm

Enzymes are used to cut the insulin-making gene out of the chromosome

The plasmid is then put back into the bacterium

The bacterium is then put into a fermentation vessel where it multiplies rapidly to form clones which all produce insulin

The plasmid is cut open using the same enzymes and the insulin-making gene is inserted

The insulin is removed and used to treat diabetes

💡 *Remember, insulin lowers blood-sugar levels and glucagon raises blood-sugar levels.*

You may be asked to provide arguments for and against the use of genetic engineering. Be prepared to discuss the benefits and the risks involved.

Human Genome Project

The **Human Genome Project** was completed in 2003. It took scientists from all around the world 10 years to complete. It aimed to identify all the genes in human DNA and study them. The benefits include improved diagnosis of disease and earlier detection of genetic diseases in families, such as breast cancer and Alzheimer's disease. The use of DNA in forensic science has improved greatly.

It is now possible to identify suspects, clear the wrongly accused, identify paternity and match organ donors with recipients. A person's 'DNA fingerprint' is unique. There is only an extremely slim chance of another person having the same 'fingerprint'. Scientists identify a region of DNA that is unique to that person and can then build up a profile.

KEY TERMS

Make sure you understand these terms before moving on!

- gene therapy
- cystic fibrosis
- GM crops
- genetic engineering
- Human Genome Project

QUICK TEST

1. What is 'genetic engineering'?
2. What are the benefits of developing crops that are resistant to frost?
3. What was the 'Human Genome Project'?
4. What are the risks of using bacteria for genetic engineering?
5. What is gene therapy?

The nervous system

The nervous system is in charge. It controls and coordinates the parts of your body so that they work together at the right time. The nervous system coordinates things you don't even think about, like breathing and blinking.

The central nervous system

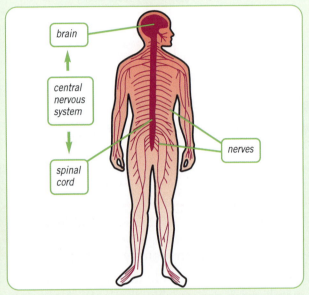

The **central nervous system** (CNS) consists of the brain and spinal cord connected to different parts of the body by **nerves**. Your body's sense organs contain **receptors**. Receptors detect changes in the environment called stimuli.

Nose – sensitive to chemicals in the air
Mouth – sensitive to chemicals in food
Ears – sensitive to sound and balance
Skin – sensitive to touch, pressure and temperature
Eyes – sensitive to light

The receptors send messages along nerves to the brain and spinal cord in response to stimuli from the environment. The messages are called **nerve impulses**. The CNS sends **nerve impulses** back along nerves to **effectors**, which bring about a response. Effectors are muscles that bring about movement, or glands that secrete hormones.

Nerves

Nerves are made up of nerve cells or **neurones**. There are three types of neurone: sensory, relay and motor.

Neurones have a nucleus, cytoplasm and cell membrane, but they have changed their shape and become specialised.

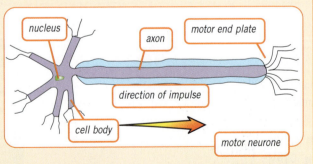

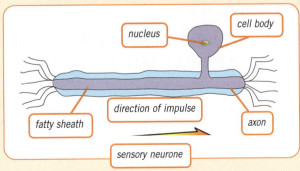

The **sensory neurones** receive messages from the receptors and send them to the CNS.

The **motor neurones** send messages from the CNS to the effectors telling them what to do. Nerve impulses travel in **one direction only**. The fatty sheath is for insulation and for speeding up nerve impulses. A **relay neurone** connects the sensory neurone to the motor neurone in the CNS.

Synapses

In between the neurones there is a gap called a **synapse**.

When an impulse reaches the end of an axon, a chemical is released. This chemical diffuses across the gap. This starts an impulse in the next neurone. Drugs and alcohol can affect synapses, slowing down or even stopping them from functioning properly.

The brain

The brain is situated at the top of the spinal cord and is protected by the skull. Together with the spinal cord and neurones, it makes up the **central nervous system**. It coordinates the different parts of the body, making them work together to bring about the correct response to a stimulus.

Parts of the brain

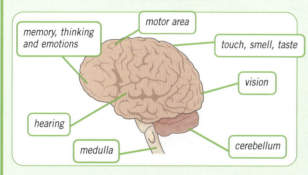

memory, thinking and emotions
motor area
touch, smell, taste
vision
hearing
medulla
cerebellum

- The cerebral cortex makes up the outer layer of the brain: in mammals, like humans, it appears to have many bumps and grooves.
- The cerebral cortex can be divided down the middle into two halves, called the cerebral hemispheres.
- The cerebral hemispheres are made up of lobes. Look at the diagram to see which areas are responsible for each function.
- The medulla is the part of the brain that attaches to the spinal cord. It controls automatic actions such as breathing and heart rate.
- The cerebellum controls our coordination and balance.

The brain and learning

The brain works by sending electrical impulses received from the sense organs to the muscles: it coordinates the response. In mammals, the brain contains billions of neurones that allow learning by experience and behaviour. The interaction between mammals and their environment results in nerve pathways forming in the brain. When you learn from experience, pathways in the brain become more likely to transmit certain impulses than others, which is why it is easier to learn through repetition.

 Look at the page on the reflex arc and link it with the brain and nervous system.

KEY TERMS

Make sure you understand these terms before moving on!

- CNS
- receptors
- nerve impulses
- effectors
- sensory neurone
- motor neurone
- relay neurone
- synapse

QUICK TEST

1. What is CNS an abbreviation for?
2. What is a synapse?
3. Which neurone is connected to receptors?
4. Which neurone is connected to the effector?
5. Which neurone connects the sensory neurone and the motor neurone?

The reflex arc

The reflex arc

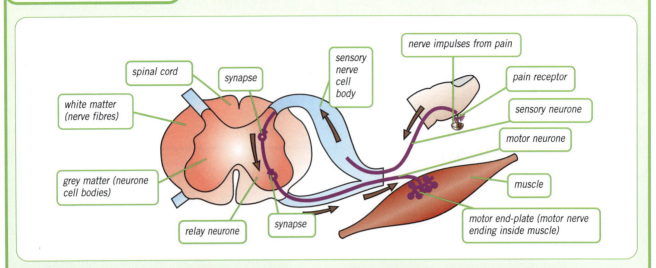

The reflex response to your CNS and back again can be shown in a diagram called **the reflex arc**.

1 The **stimulus** in this example is a sharp object.
2 The receptor is the pain sensor in the skin.
3 The nerve impulse travels along the sensory neurone.
4 The impulse is passed across a synapse to the relay neurone.
5 The impulse is passed across a synapse to the motor neurone.
6 The impulse is passed across a synapse to the muscle effector in the arm.
7 You move your hand away.

The reflex arc can be shown in a **block diagram**:

stimulus → receptor → sensory neurone → relay neurone → motor neurone → effector → response

 Make sure that you learn the diagram of the reflex arc and the block diagram. Either one may come up in the exam.

Reactions

You can see how quick your reflexes are by measuring your **reaction** times. One way to do this is to place your arm on a bench with your hand out as if holding an imaginary cup. A partner holds a long ruler above your hand. When your partner drops the ruler, you must try to catch it as quickly as possible. Repeat the test 10 times to see if your reaction time improves with practice. You are only using your sight with this test. You could also try the test with the ruler touching your hand, so you are using your touch sense as well as your sight, or blindfolded and your partner lets you know when they are going to drop the ruler so you are only using your hearing sense. This way you are using senses other than sight to test your reaction times.

Reflex and voluntary actions

Voluntary actions are things you have to think about: they are under our conscious control. They must be learned, like talking or writing.

Reflex actions produce rapid involuntary responses and often protect us and other animals from harm. Examples include reflex actions in a newborn baby, the pupils' response to light, the knee-jerk reflex and blinking.

Simple reflex actions help animals survive as they respond to a stimulus such as smelling and finding food or avoiding predators. The action of ducking when objects travel too close to the head and moving parts of the body away from pain helps to protect us.

In certain circumstances, the brain can override a reflex response. For example, when you pick up a hot plate, the brain sends a message to the motor neurone in the reflex arc to keep hold of the plate rather than drop it.

A reflex response to a new situation can be learned. This is called **conditioning** and involves a secondary stimulus. For example, the smell of food makes dogs produce saliva.

 Learn examples that follow the reflex arc: for example, touching a hot object or getting dust trapped in your eye.

KEY TERMS

Make sure you understand these terms before moving on!

- reflex arc
- stimulus
- reaction
- voluntary action
- reflex action

QUICK TEST

1. Where in your body might you find a relay neurone?

2. How many synapses are there in a typical reflex arc?

3. What has to happen before a reflex arc can occur?

4. Is blinking a reflex action?

5. Why do we have reflex actions?

6. What is the difference between a reflex action and a voluntary action?

7. Do you think you can stop reflex actions? Provide an example situation.

8. Which comes first in a reflex arc, the receptor or the effector?

9. Which neurone passes the nerve impulse to the effector?

10. Which neurone receives the nerve impulse from the receptor?

Hormones

Hormones are chemicals released from glands in the body straight into the bloodstream to the target organs. The effects of hormones are slower than nervous messages but longer lasting. They control things that need constant adjustment.

The menstrual cycle

The menstrual cycle lasts approximately 28 days. It consists of a menstrual bleed and ovulation, the release of an egg. Hormones control the whole cycle. Ovaries secrete the hormones **progesterone** and **oestrogen**.

 The role of the hormones in controlling the menstrual cycle is a favourite for the exam.

Days 1–5 – a menstrual bleed (a period) occurs. The lining of the uterus breaks down. This is caused by **lack of progesterone**

Days 5–14 – oestrogen is released from the ovaries, which causes the uterus lining to thicken. Oestrogen also stimulates egg development and release of the egg from the ovaries, called **ovulation**

Days 14–28 – progesterone is released, which maintains the uterus lining. If no fertilisation occurs then progesterone production stops

Days 28–5 – the cycle begins again

Controlling fertility

Fertility in women can be controlled in two ways.

1 FSH can be administered as a '**fertility drug**' to women whose own production is too low to stimulate eggs to mature. This can result in multiple births.
2 Oestrogen can be used as an oral contraceptive to inhibit FSH, so that no eggs mature.

The pituitary gland

The two hormones released from the ovaries are in fact controlled by the **pituitary gland**, which is situated at the base of the brain. The pituitary gland secretes two more hormones, the follicle stimulating hormone (FSH) and the luteinising hormone (LH).

FSH stimulates eggs to mature and causes the release of oestrogen from the ovary. Oestrogen inhibits further release of FSH. The release of LH stimulates ovulation and the release of progesterone.

IVF

In vitro fertilisation (**IVF**) is a treatment for infertile couples. It involves extracting the eggs and sperm, then fertilising them outside the body. The cells that develop are then implanted in the womb for growth and development into an embryo.

FSH is the hormone used to stimulate egg production. IVF is a relatively expensive process and is not always successful. Some areas of the country offer the initial IVF treatment on the National Health: subsequent rounds must be paid for. There are some social and ethical consequences associated with the practice of IVF,

particularly its use on older couples. Some clinics set an upper age limit on couples they will treat, as they feel the chances of success fall with increasing age. There is also the possibility that birth defects increase with older eggs.

IVF can also create many fertilised embryos. There is then the question of what should be done with the embryos not implanted back in the womb. Some couples may look at freezing them for later use, but what should happen to the remainder? Should they be thrown away or used for medical research?

The pancreas and homeostasis

Homeostasis is the mechanism by which the body maintains normal levels such as temperature and control of body water by making constant adjustments. The **pancreas** is one of the organs involved in homeostasis: it maintains the level of glucose (sugar) in the blood so that there is enough for respiration. The pancreas secretes two hormones into the blood, **insulin** and **glucagon**. If blood-sugar levels are too high, which could be the case after a high carbohydrate meal, special cells in the pancreas detect these changes and release insulin. The liver responds to the amount of insulin in the blood, takes up glucose and stores it as glycogen. Blood-sugar levels then return to normal.

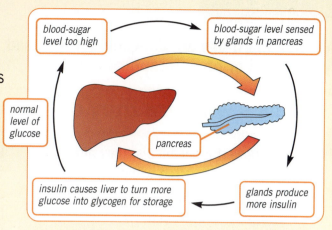

If blood-sugar levels are too low, which could be the case during exercise, the pancreas secretes glucagon. Glucagon stimulates the conversion of stored glycogen in the liver back into glucose which is released into the blood. Blood-sugar levels return to normal.

Diabetes

Diabetes results when the **pancreas does not make enough of the hormone insulin** and sometimes none at all. As a consequence blood-sugar levels rise and very little glucose is absorbed by the cells for respiration. This can make the sufferer tired and thirsty. If untreated, it leads to weight loss and even death.

Diabetes can be controlled in two ways:

1 Attention to diet – a special low-glucose diet can be all that is needed to control some diabetes.
2 In more severe cases, diabetics have to inject themselves with insulin before meals. This causes the liver to convert the glucose into glycogen straight away.

KEY TERMS

Make sure you understand these terms before moving on!

- hormones
- progesterone
- oestrogen
- fertility drug
- pituitary gland
- IVF
- pancreas
- glucagon
- diabetes
- insulin

QUICK TEST

1. How are hormones transported around the body?
2. Where are the hormones oestrogen and progesterone made?
3. Which two hormones are produced by the pituitary gland?
4. What is homeostasis?
5. What does the liver do with excess glucose?
6. Which hormone raises blood-sugar levels?
7. Which hormone lowers blood-sugar levels?
8. How can diabetes be treated?

Drugs

Alcohol and drugs are dangerous if misused, for either recreational or pharmaceutical purposes.

Drugs – why are they dangerous?

Drugs are powerful chemicals: they alter the way the body works, often without you realising it. They can quickly become an **addiction**: people become dependent on drugs and suffer withdrawal symptoms without them. Even useful drugs, such as penicillin and antibiotics, can be dangerous if misused.

Drugs affect the brain and nervous system. Some drugs are taken for recreational purposes and are illegal: others, such as alcohol and tobacco, are legal. The overall impact on our health of legal drugs can be greater, as more people take them than illegal drugs. Drugs fall into four main groups: sedatives, painkillers, hallucinogens and stimulants.

Sedatives

Sedatives slow down the brain and nervous system and make you feel sleepy. Examples are tranquillisers and sleeping pills. They are often given to people suffering from anxiety and stress. These drugs seriously alter reaction times and give you poor judgement of speed and distances.

Hallucinogens

These drugs **make you see or hear things that don't exist**. These are called hallucinations. Ecstasy, LSD and cannabis are examples of hallucinogens. The hallucinations can lead to fatal accidents.

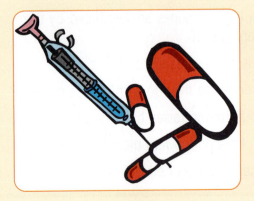

Painkillers

These drugs **suppress the pain sensors in the brain**. Examples are **paracetamol**, aspirin, heroin and morphine. Heroin can be injected, which can increase the risk of contracting HIV; it is also highly addictive.

Painkillers reduce fever and relieve pain with virtually no side effects. The recommended dosage of paracetamol is 8 × 500 mg tablets in 24 hours. Taking 24–30 tablets within 24 hours is considered to be an overdose, and this quantity is lowered if the tablets are taken in combination with other medication or alcohol or if the user's weight is low. An overdose may not be apparent for 24 hours until the user begins to suffer from jaundice (a yellowing of the skin), confusion and eventually loses consciousness. Death occurs through liver failure and is extremely painful. For maximum recovery to occur, an antidote must be administered within 12 to 24 hours. There are approximately 130 deaths each year in England and Wales from paracetamol overdose.

Stimulants

Stimulants **speed up the brain and nervous system:** they make you feel more alert and awake. Amphetamines, cocaine and the less harmful caffeine in tea and

coffee are examples. Dependence on this type of drug is high and withdrawing use causes serious **depression**.

Drugs and the law

Cannabis has recently has become a class C drug, carrying less harsh penalties for those caught in possession of the drug. If, however, the user also intends to supply other users, the penalty is up to 14 years' imprisonment.

The debate still continues about whether cannabis is harmful and addictive, and whether it leads on to harder drugs such as heroin. At present, health professionals cannot agree. It is said to be psychologically addictive, however, and if taken with nicotine,

the nicotine makes it physically addictive. Recent research indicates that the use of cannabis can lead to depression and mental illness in later life.

Cannabinoid drugs (the active part of cannabis) can be used to treat pain but some say that these drugs are no more effective than conventional treatments and can have undesirable side effects. Evidence supporting the pain-relieving properties of cannabis is largely anecdotal. Some medical studies claim that these drugs relieve pain by interfering directly with pain signalling in the nervous system. Others argue that cannabinoids reduce anxiety, create euphoria and have sedative affects, and that it is the combination of these factors that create the impression of pain relief. Some people argue that it is a useful pain relief drug for the terminally ill, where long-term risk is not a concern. Medical opinion, however, fluctuates.

KEY TERMS

Make sure you understand these terms before moving on!
- addiction
- sedatives
- paracetamol
- stimulants
- depression
- cannabinoids

QUICK TEST

1. How do sedatives work?
2. What drug class is cannabis?
3. What makes cannabis physically addictive?
4. How many paracetamol tablets are considered to be an overdose?
5. What type of drug speeds up the nervous system?
6. What is the maximum number of paracetamol tablets that should be taken over 24 hours?
7. What is paracetamol used for?
8. How do stimulants affect the nervous system?
9. Why shouldn't you take sedatives before driving?
10. How do painkillers work?

Solvents, alcohol and tobacco

There is no doubt that smoking and solvents damage our health. In excess, alcohol can also cause health problems and its effects can be harmful, even in small doses.

Solvents

Solvents include everyday products like glue and aerosols. Solvent fumes are inhaled and are absorbed by the lungs. They soon reach the brain and **slow down breathing and heart rates**. Solvents also damage the **kidneys and liver**. Repeated inhalation can cause loss of control and unconsciousness. Many first-time inhalers die from heart failure or suffocation if using aerosols. Many of the symptoms are likened to being drunk. The user may also vomit, and not appear to be in control of their actions.

Alcohol

Alcohol is a depressant and reduces the activity of the brain and nervous system. It is absorbed through the gut and taken up to the brain in the blood. Alcohol damages neurones in the brain and can cause irreversible brain damage. The liver breaks down alcohol at a rate of one unit an hour but an excess of alcohol has a very **damaging effect on the liver called cirrhosis.** Increasing amounts of alcohol causes people to lose control and slur their words. In this state, accidents are more likely to happen. Drinking can be very addictive, without the person realising they have a problem.

1 glass of wine

$\frac{1}{2}$ pint cider (0.3 litre)

1 glass sherry

$\frac{1}{2}$ pint beer (0.3 litre)

1 single whisky

All these drinks contain one unit of alcohol

Smoking

Tobacco causes health problems. It contains many harmful chemicals: **nicotine** is an addictive substance and a mild stimulant, **tar** is known to contain carcinogens that contribute to cancer and carbon monoxide prevents the red blood cells from carrying oxygen. If pregnant women smoke, **carbon monoxide** deprives the foetus of oxygen and can lead to a low birth mass. Some of the diseases aggravated by smoking include **emphysema, bronchitis, heart and blood vessel problems** and lung cancer.

As well as the health problems it causes, smoking is also extremely expensive and is now considered to be anti-social. There are moves towards a complete ban of smoking in public places. Do you think it will ever happen?

Addiction

Drugs, solvents, alcohol and tobacco can all become **chemically or psychologically addictive**. In the process of chemical addiction, the body gets used to the drug (becomes **tolerant**) and the user must take an increasing amount of the drug for it to continue to have an effect. If a person stops taking the drug, they will develop **withdrawal symptoms** such as fever, nausea and hallucinations.

When a person becomes psychologically addicted to a drug, they simply feel that they must keep on taking the drug, but will not experience harmful effects if they stop.

Scientific concept

The link between smoking and lung cancer is now widely accepted. Tobacco contains carcinogens, the chemicals that cause cancer. According to Cancer Research UK, smoking causes nine out of ten lung cancers.

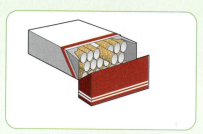

KEY TERMS

Make sure you understand these terms before moving on!

- depressant
- cirrhosis
- carbon monoxide
- lung cancer
- withdrawal symptoms

SOLVENTS, ALCOHOL AND TOBACCO

Biology

QUICK TEST

1. Which parts of the body are affected by alcohol?
2. Approximately how long does it take the body to break down one unit of alcohol?
3. Name three chemicals which tobacco contains.
4. What diseases does smoking cause?
5. What is the name of the disease of the liver?
6. What chemical does tar contain?
7. What are 'withdrawal symptoms'?
8. Why should pregnant women avoid smoking?
9. Which chemical in tobacco causes cancer?
10. What causes tolerance of a drug?

Causes of disease

Microbes are bacteria, fungi and viruses. Not all microbes cause disease: some are useful. Microbes that get inside you and make you feel ill are called *pathogens* or germs. Pathogens rapidly reproduce in warm conditions when there is plenty of food.

How are diseases spread?

Diseases are spread:

- through **contact** with infected people, animals or objects used by infected people, e.g. athlete's foot, chicken pox and measles
- through the **air**, e.g. flu, colds and pneumonia
- through infected **food and drink**, e.g. cholera from infected drinking water and salmonella food-poisoning.

Disease can be non-infectious and caused by vitamin deficiencies such as scurvy (lack of vitamin C), mineral deficiencies such as anaemia (lack of iron), or bodily disorders like cancer or diabetes. Other disorders can be inherited, like red-green colour blindness or diabetes.

 Remember that not all microbes are harmful and cause disease.

Bacteria

Bacteria are living organisms that feed, move and carry out respiration. They reproduce rapidly to produce exact copies of themselves.

How bacteria cause disease

Bacteria cause disease by destroying living tissue: for example, tuberculosis destroys lung tissue. Bacteria can also produce poisons, called **toxins**: for example, food poisoning is caused by bacteria releasing **toxins**.

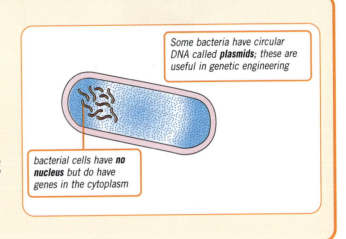

*Some bacteria have circular DNA called **plasmids**; these are useful in genetic engineering*

*bacterial cells have **no nucleus** but do have genes in the cytoplasm*

Viruses

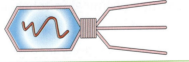

Viruses consist of a protein coat surrounding a few genes

Viruses are much smaller than bacteria. They don't feed, move, respire or grow: they just reproduce. Viruses can only survive inside the cells of a living organism. They **reproduce inside the cells** and release thousands of new viruses to infect new cells. They **kill the cell** in the process.

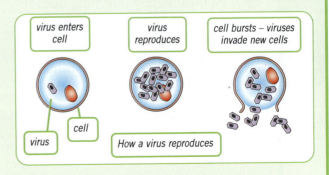

virus enters cell

virus reproduces

cell bursts – viruses invade new cells

virus   *cell*   *How a virus reproduces*

Examples of diseases caused by viruses are HIV, flu, chicken pox and measles.

Fungi

Fungi cause diseases such as athlete's foot and ringworm. Fungi reproduce by **making spores** that can be carried from person to person. Most fungi are useful as decomposers. Yeast is a fungus that is used when making bread, beer and wine.

Vectors

Some pathogens rely on **vectors** to transfer them from one organism to another. A vector is an organism that transports a pathogen. An example would be a mosquito. A mosquito carrying the parasite that causes malaria may infect another person by injecting the parasite into the person's bloodstream when it bites them.

How do pathogens get in?

Pathogens have to enter our body before they can do any harm.

respiratory system – droplets of moisture containing viruses are breathed in

digestive system – pathogens can enter via your food and drink

skin – if the skin is damaged, pathogens can get in

reproductive system – diseases can be passed on through sexual intercourse

KEY TERMS

Make sure you understand these terms before moving on!

- microbes
- pathogens
- bacteria
- toxins
- viruses
- vectors

Symptoms of infection

Symptoms are the effects diseases have on the body: they are usually caused by the toxins released by the pathogens. Symptoms include a high temperature, headache, loss of appetite and sickness.

QUICK TEST

1. Name the three types of microbes.
2. What do we call microbes that cause disease?
3. Why should you be careful in countries that have mosquitoes?
4. How do viruses cause disease?
5. Give two examples of diseases caused by fungi.
6. Why should you wash your hands regularly?
7. What is a vector? Give an example.
8. Name three ways in which pathogens can enter the body.
9. If you had measles, would a virus or a bacterium have infected you?
10. Name two diseases caused by bacteria.

Defence against disease

Prevention is better than cure

The human body has several ways of preventing disease-causing microbes from entering. This is the body's **first line of defence**:

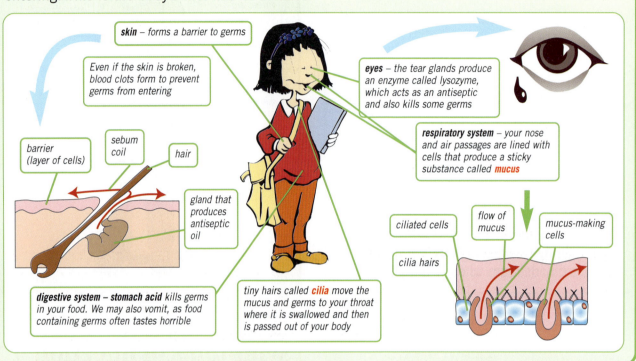

skin – forms a barrier to germs

Even if the skin is broken, blood clots form to prevent germs from entering

barrier (layer of cells)

sebum coil

hair

gland that produces antiseptic oil

digestive system – stomach acid kills germs in your food. We may also vomit, as food containing germs often tastes horrible

tiny hairs called **cilia** move the mucus and germs to your throat where it is swallowed and then is passed out of your body

eyes – the tear glands produce an enzyme called lysozyme, which acts as an antiseptic and also kills some germs

respiratory system – your nose and air passages are lined with cells that produce a sticky substance called **mucus**

ciliated cells

flow of mucus

mucus-making cells

cilia hairs

The immune system response

If pathogens get into the body, white blood cells travelling around in your blood spring into action. White blood cells can make chemicals called antitoxins that destroy the toxins produced by bacteria. White blood cells called **phagocytes** try to engulf bacteria or viruses before they have a chance to do any harm. This is the body's **second line of defence** and is **non-specific**. If, however, there are large numbers of pathogens, another type of white blood cell, called a **lymphocyte**, is involved. This is the **third line of defence** and is called the **specific immune system**. All germs have chemicals on their surface called antigens. Lymphocytes recognise these antigens as foreign. Lymphocytes produce chemicals called antibodies that attach to these antigens and clump them together. Phagocytes can then engulf and destroy the bacteria and viruses. Antibodies are made specifically to fight a particular antigen, which is why this is referred to as the **specific immune response**.

Natural immunity

Making antibodies takes time which is why you feel ill at first, and then get better as the disease is destroyed by the white blood cells. Once a particular antibody is made it stays in your body. If the same disease enters your body the antibodies are much quicker at destroying it and you feel no symptoms. **You are now immune to that disease**.

Tuberculosis

Tuberculosis or TB is an infectious disease affecting the lungs, which results in bacteria destroying the lung tissue. It is spread when sufferers of the disease cough and sneeze, causing other people to breathe in the bacterial TB. TB was a major problem in the nineteenth and early twentieth centuries. In the 1940s, improvements in public health and the discovery of an antibiotic in 1946 to treat TB led to a decline in the spread of the infection. For a while, however, the guard was let down, there was less of a focus on hygiene and incidences of the disease increased again in the 1980s, particularly as drug-resistant strains began to emerge.

There are about 7000 reported cases in the UK at the present time. Treatment involves a six-month course of antibiotics, and various antibiotics are used to prevent the bacteria becoming resistant to one type. A vaccine called the BCG is also given at schools to prevent people catching TB.

Artificial immunity

Artificial immunity involves the use of **vaccines (immunisations). A vaccine contains dead or harmless germs**. These germs still have antigens in them and your white blood cells respond to them as if they were alive by multiplying and producing antibodies. A vaccine provides our bodies with an advanced warning so that if a specific germ infects a person, the white blood cells can **respond immediately** and kill it.

Antibiotics

Sometimes bacteria get through the body's defences and reproduce successfully. Antibiotics can kill the germs without harming the body's cells. Penicillin was the first form of antibiotic. It is made from a mould called *penicillium notatum*. **Antibiotics cannot treat infections caused by viruses**. The body has to fight them on its own. Antibiotics can kill most bacteria, but as we continue to use them, bacteria are becoming **resistant** to them. New antibiotics are constantly needed to fight the battle against bacteria.

 Ways of preventing infection often come up in the exam. Do make sure that you know how the body prevents infection from getting in and causing disease.

KEY TERMS

Make sure you understand these terms before moving on!

- mucus
- cilia
- immune system response
- phagocyte
- lymphocyte
- natural immunity
- artificial immunity
- antibiotics
- penicillin

QUICK TEST

1. What was the first form of antibiotic called?
2. Name the two types of white blood cell that are involved in the immune response.
3. How do phagocytes kill germs?
4. Which chemicals do white blood cells produce?
5. Why do you tend to get some diseases, like measles, only once?
6. How does the body recognise foreign bacteria and viruses?

Practice questions

Use the questions to test your progress. Check your answers on page 110.

1 Which organ in the body coordinates our response to stimuli?

....

2 Why is making antibodies known as the 'specific immune response'?

....

3 Which organ is affected by TB?

....

4 Where in the body is insulin made?

....

5 What vaccine is used to prevent TB?

....

6 Smoking during pregnancy is harmful to the foetus in what particular way?

....

7 Where can the dodo be found?

....

8 How can insulin be made outside the body?

....

9 If you are bitten by a mosquito, what disease might you contract?

....

10 What do the letters CNS stand for and what does it consist of?

....

11 Name the three types of neurone.

....

12 If you were unable to make insulin, what disease would result?

....

13 How are hormones carried around the body?

....

14 Why is it necessary to vaccinate against flu every year?

....

15 Why isn't there a vaccine for HIV?

....

16 Explain what a vector is and give an example.

....

17 Name the two types of white blood cell that protect us from disease.

....

18 Explain the term 'natural immunity'.

....

....

19 Define the word 'homeostasis'.

....

....

20 How long ago was the theory of evolution first stated?

....

21 What are alternative forms of a gene called?

....

22 Which hormones are involved in the menstrual cycle?

....

23 What type of organisms do we use for genetic engineering?

....

24 Can penicillin be used to treat measles?

....

25 Who developed the theory of evolution that we use today?

....

26 Who developed an alternative theory of evolution based on observations of giraffes?

....

27 Why doesn't a food chain go on forever?

....

....

28 In a food chain, does the number of prey control the number of predators, or does the number of predators control the number of prey?

....

29 What is an alternative to intensive farming?

....

30 Where in your body would you find the chemical DNA?

....

Atoms and elements

Elements are made of only one type of atom.

What is in an atom?

An atom consists of a central **nucleus** surrounded by shells of electrons. The nucleus consists of protons and neutrons. Atoms of the same element have the same number of protons.

How can atoms join together?
Atoms can join together by:

- sharing electrons
- giving and taking electrons.

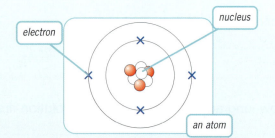

electron

nucleus

an atom

Compounds consist of two or more different types of atom that have been chemically combined.

The periodic table

Elements are often displayed in the **periodic table**. In the periodic table, elements with similar properties are found in the same vertical column. These columns are called groups. The horizontal rows in the periodic table are called periods.

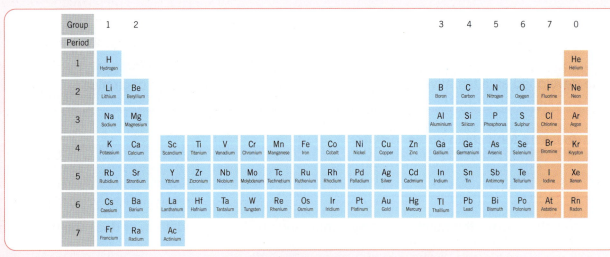

Group	1	2											3	4	5	6	7	0
Period																		
1	H Hydrogen																	He Helium
2	Li Lithium	Be Beryllium											B Boron	C Carbon	N Nitrogen	O Oxygen	F Fluorine	Ne Neon
3	Na Sodium	Mg Magnesium											Al Aluminium	Si Silicon	P Phosphorus	S Sulphur	Cl Chlorine	Ar Argon
4	K Potassium	Ca Calcium	Sc Scandium	Ti Titanium	V Vanadium	Cr Chromium	Mn Manganese	Fe Iron	Co Cobalt	Ni Nickel	Cu Copper	Zn Zinc	Ga Gallium	Ge Germanium	As Arsenic	Se Selenium	Br Bromine	Kr Krypton
5	Rb Rubidium	Sr Strontium	Y Yttrium	Zr Zirconium	Nb Niobium	Mo Molybdenum	Tc Technetium	Ru Ruthenium	Rh Rhodium	Pd Palladium	Ag Silver	Cd Cadmium	In Indium	Sn Tin	Sb Antimony	Te Tellurium	I Iodine	Xe Xenon
6	Cs Caesium	Ba Barium	La Lanthanum	Hf Hafnium	Ta Tantalum	W Tungsten	Re Rhenium	Os Osmium	Ir Iridium	Pt Platinum	Au Gold	Hg Mercury	Tl Thallium	Pb Lead	Bi Bismuth	Po Polonium	At Astatine	Rn Radon
7	Fr Francium	Ra Radium	Ac Actinium															

Metallic elements are found on the left-hand side of the periodic table.
Non-metallic elements are found on the right-hand side of the periodic table.

Symbols 1

In science, elements can be represented by **symbols**. Each element has its own unique **symbol** which is recognised all over the world. Each symbol consists of one or two letters and is much easier to read and write than the full name.

In some cases, the symbol for an element is simply the first letter of the element's name. This letter must be a capital letter.

The element **i**odine is represented by the symbol I.

I

Symbols 2

Sometimes several elements have names which start with the same letter. When this happens, we use the first letter of the element's name together with another letter from the name. The first letter is a capital and the second letter is lower case.

The element **ma**gnesium is represented by the symbol Mg.

The element **m**a**n**ganese is represented by the symbol Mn.

Sometimes an element may take its symbol from its old Latin name. When this happens the first letter is a capital and the second letter, if there is one, is lower case.

The element mercury is represented by the symbol Hg. This comes from the Latin name for mercury which is **h**ydrar**g**yrum, meaning 'liquid silver'.

Hg

Chemical reactions

Equations can be used to sum up what happens during a chemical reaction. When magnesium burns in air, the magnesium atoms react with oxygen molecules to form the compound magnesium oxide. This reaction can be summed up in the word equation:

magnesium + oxygen ➡ magnesium oxide

Chemical formula

A compound can be represented using a chemical **formula**. The formula shows the type and ratio of the atoms that are joined together in the compound.

Ammonia has the chemical formula **NH$_3$**.

This shows that in ammonia, nitrogen and hydrogen, atoms are joined together in the ratio of one nitrogen atom to three hydrogen atoms.

Why do we have to take care when writing symbols?

The element carbon has the symbol C.
The element oxygen has the symbol O.
The element cobalt has the symbol Co.

The formula CO shows that a carbon atom and an oxygen atom have been chemically combined in a one-to-one ratio. This is the formula of the compound carbon monoxide.

The symbol Co represents the element cobalt. Notice how the second letter of the symbol is written in lower case. If it wasn't, we would have a completely different substance.

The formula CO$_2$ shows that carbon and oxygen atoms have been chemically combined in a one-to-two ratio. This is the formula of the compound carbon dioxide.

As you can see, we need to be very careful when we write chemical symbols and formulae.

KEY TERMS

Make sure you understand these terms before moving on!
- nucleus
- compounds
- periodic table
- symbols
- formula

QUICK TEST

1. What is the centre of an atom called?

2. What is special about elements?

3. How can atoms join together?

4. Give the chemical symbol of the element oxygen.

5. Give the name of the element with the symbol Na.

6. Water has the formula H$_2$O. What does this formula tell us?

The periodic table

As the *elements* were discovered, early chemists tried to find patterns among them, but they struggled to find links.

The history of the periodic table

1864 John Newlands

Newlands arranged the known elements in rows of seven using their atomic mass. He noticed that there were similarities between every eighth element (the noble gases were not discovered until later). Newlands had identified **periodicity**. He did not leave gaps for elements that had not yet been discovered, however, so many problems developed.

1869 Dimitri Mendeleev

Mendeleev ordered the elements using their atomic masses (as Newlands had before him), but realised that some elements had not yet been discovered. **Mendeleev left gaps** for these new elements. In addition, he was able to predict the properties of the missing elements. When these elements were eventually discovered and found to have the properties that Mendeleev had predicted, his idea was proved right.

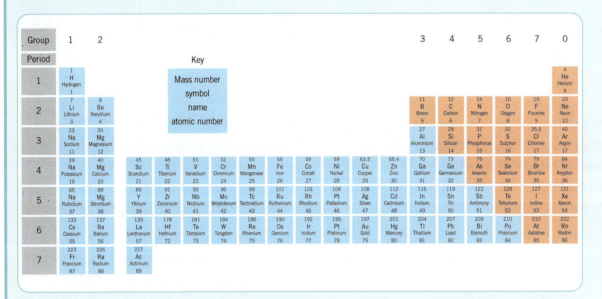

Mendeleev made another big breakthrough when he decided not to stick too strictly to the order of increasing atomic mass. When similar elements did not line up in the right way he **swapped the order** around.

He looked at tellurium and iodine, for example. Tellurium atoms have a higher mass than iodine atoms. The properties of both elements, however, suggest that tellurium would be better placed in Group 6 and iodine would be better placed in Group 7. So Mendeleev swapped them over. Although protons had not yet been discovered, by lining up the elements in this way, Mendeleev had actually put the **atoms in order of increasing atomic number**, or increasing number of protons.

 Practise using the periodic table to find the symbols for different elements.

The modern periodic table

In the modern periodic table, elements are arranged in order of **increasing atomic number**. It is called a periodic table because elements with similar properties occur at regular intervals or 'periodically'.

The elements are placed in horizontal rows called **periods** so that elements with similar properties are in the same column. These vertical columns are called **groups**. The groups may sometimes be numbered using Roman numerals, for example, Group 1 may be written as Group I.

The elements in Group 1 include lithium, sodium and potassium. All the elements in Group 1 of the periodic table share similar properties: they are all metals and they all consist of atoms which have just one electron in their outer shell. When these metals react they form ions which have a 1^+ charge.

Elements in the same period have the same number of shells of electrons.

⚠ *Elements in the same group of the periodic table have similar properties because they have the same number of electrons in their outer shells.*

KEY TERMS

Make sure you understand these terms before moving on!

- elements
- periodicity
- atomic number
- periods
- groups

QUICK TEST

1. How did Newlands arrange the elements?
2. Which element did Newlands place in the same group as lithium?
3. Why did Newlands' method develop problems?
4. How did Mendeleev's ideas differ from Newlands' ideas?
5. Why did Mendeleev place tellurium before iodine?
6. How is the modern periodic table arranged?
7. What are the vertical columns in the periodic table called?
8. How many electrons are there in the outer shell of the members of Group 1?
9. How many electrons are there in the outer shell of the members of Group 3?
10. What are the horizontal rows in the periodic table called?

Transition metals

Metallic bonding

Metals have a giant structure. In metals, the **electrons** in the highest energy shells (outer electrons) are not bound to one atom but are free to move through the whole structure. This means that metals consist of positive metal ions surrounded by a sea of negative electrons. **Metallic bonding** is the attraction between these ions and the electrons.

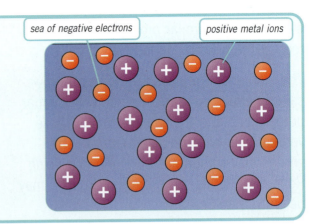

sea of negative electrons

positive metal ions

Properties of metals 1

Metallic bonding means that metals have several very useful properties:

- The free electrons mean that metals are **good electrical conductors**.
- The free electrons also mean that metals are **good thermal conductors**.

- The strong attraction between the metal ions and the electrons means that metals can be drawn into **wires** as the ions slide over each other.
- Metals can also be **hammered into shape**.

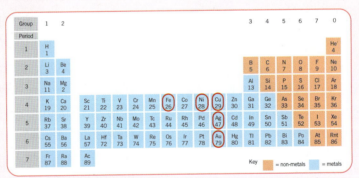

The transition metals are found in the middle section of the periodic table. Copper, iron and nickel are examples of very useful transition metals. All transition metals have characteristic properties. They:

- have **high melting points** (except for mercury, which is a liquid at room temperature)
- have **high densities**
- form coloured compounds.

They are also strong, tough and hard-wearing. All transition metals are much less reactive than Group 1 metals. They all react much

less vigorously with oxygen and water. Many transition metals can **form ions with different charges**. This makes transition metals useful catalysts for many reactions.

Copper

- Copper is a good electrical and thermal conductor.
- It can be easily bent into new shapes and does not corrode.
- Copper is widely used in electrical wiring.
- It is also used to make water pipes.

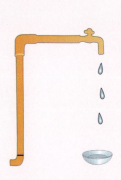

Properties of metals 2

Iron

- Iron, made in a blast furnace, is strong but brittle.
- Iron is often made into steel.
- Steel is strong and cheap. It is used in vast quantities. It is also heavy and may rust, however.
- Iron and steel are useful structural materials. They are used to make buildings, bridges, ships, cars and trains.
- Iron is used as a catalyst in the Haber process.

Gold

- Gold is rare and this makes it valuable.
- Gold is shiny and unreactive but too soft for many uses.
- Gold can be mixed with other metals.
- It is widely used to make jewellery.

Silver

- Silver is shiny and quite unreactive.
- It has the highest electrical and thermal conductivity of any metal.
- It is used to make coins, jewellery and cutlery.

Metal alloys

Alloys are made by mixing metals together.
Common alloys include:

- amalgams – which are mainly mercury
- brass – which is made from copper and zinc
- bronze – which is made from copper and tin
- solder – which is made from lead and tin
- steel – which is mainly iron.

Occasionally, alloys can even be made by mixing metals with non-metals. This is true for the alloy steel which is made from iron and the non-metal carbon.

KEY TERMS

Make sure you understand these terms before moving on!

- electrons
- metallic bonding
- electrical conductor
- thermal conductor
- alloys

QUICK TEST

1. Why are metals able to conduct heat and electricity?
2. In which part of the periodic table are the transition metals found?
3. What are the characteristics of transition metals?
4. Why is copper used for electrical wiring?
5. Why is copper used for water pipes?
6. Why is iron made into steel?
7. Which items can be made from steel?
8. In which process is iron used as a catalyst?
9. Why is gold valuable?
10. Why is gold not used to make tools?

Group 1 – The alkali metals

The Group 1 metals are found on the far left-hand side of the periodic table.

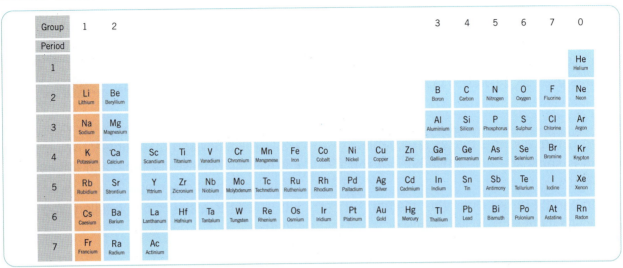

Reactions of the Group 1 metals with water

The metals lithium, sodium and potassium are all **less dense than water**. If these metals are placed in water they will float. All Group 1 metals react with water to produce hydrogen gas and an alkaline solution of a metal hydroxide.

Lithium

Lithium reacts with water to produce a solution of lithium hydroxide and hydrogen gas. We can test for the presence of hydrogen gas by placing a lighted splint nearby. If hydrogen is present it will burn with a squeaky pop.

lithium

lithium + water ➡ lithium hydroxide + hydrogen

Sodium

Sodium reacts more vigorously with water to produce a solution of sodium hydroxide and hydrogen gas. The sodium metal moves around on the surface of the water as it reacts. If **universal indicator** is added to the solution of sodium hydroxide that is made during this reaction, it will turn **purple**.

sodium

sodium + water ➡ sodium hydroxide + hydrogen

Potassium

Potassium is the most reactive of the three metals. The reaction between potassium and water is so **vigorous** that the hydrogen gas produced may ignite and burn with a lilac flame.

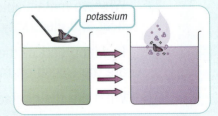

potassium

potassium + water ➡ potassium hydroxide + hydrogen

From these descriptions we can see that chemical reactions happen at different rates.

 Alkali metals are so reactive that they must be stored under oil to stop them reacting with moisture or oxygen in the air.

Why do Group 1 metals react in a similar way?

- The alkali metals are **all very reactive**.
- Alkali metals have just one electron in their outer shell which they want to give away.
- Group 1 metals have similar properties because they have similar electron structures.
- Alkali metals **react with non-metals to form ionic compounds**. For example, sodium reacts with chlorine to form sodium chloride:

  sodium + chlorine ➡ sodium chloride

- When they react, alkali metal atoms lose their outer electrons to form ions with a 1$^+$ charge.
- Group 1 metals form white compounds which dissolve to form colourless solutions.

Why does potassium react more vigorously than lithium?

- Reactivity increases down the group.
- As we progress down the group, the outer electron is further away from the nucleus. Therefore, **it is easier for atoms to lose their outer electron**.

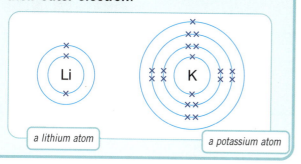

a lithium atom   *a potassium atom*

KEY TERMS

Make sure you understand these terms before moving on!

- dense
- universal indicator
- vigorous
- reactive
- ionic

QUICK TEST

1. Name the first three metals in Group 1.

2. How many electrons are present in the outer shell of all Group 1 metals?

3. Why do all the Group 1 metals have similar properties?

4. What type of compounds do Group 1 metals form?

5. What charge do Group 1 ions have?

6. What is the trend in reactivity down Group 1 of the periodic table?

7. Why does sodium float on water?

8. What is the test for hydrogen gas?

9. Give the word equation for the reaction between sodium and water.

10. Give the word equation for the reaction between potassium and chlorine.

Group 7 and Group 0

Group 7 and Group 0 are found on the right-hand side of the periodic table. They are all non-metals.

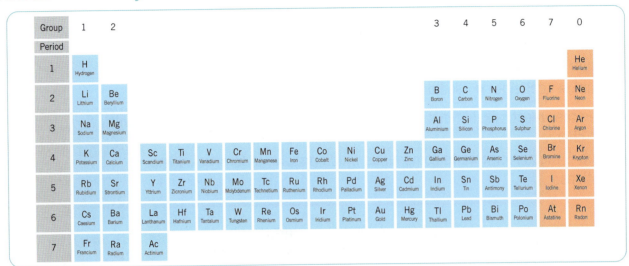

Why do halogens react in a similar way?

Halogens have seven electrons in their outer shell. They react with metal atoms to form **ionic compounds**. For example, chlorine reacts with calcium to form calcium chloride:

chlorine + calcium ➡ calcium chloride

When they react, halogen atoms gain an electron to form ions with a 1⁻ charge.

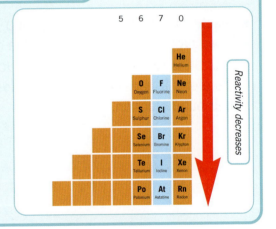

Displacement reactions involving halogens

The reactivity of the halogens decreases down the group. The most reactive halogen is fluorine, followed by chlorine, bromine and then iodine. **A more reactive halogen will displace a less reactive halogen from its solution.** Hence chlorine could displace bromine or iodine. While bromine could displace iodine it could not displace chlorine, however.

For example, chlorine will displace iodine from a solution of potassium iodide:

potassium iodide + chlorine ➡ potassium chloride + iodine

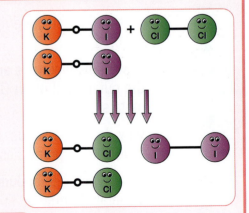

❗ *Elements in Group 7 have similar properties and react with metals to form compounds in which the Group 7 ion carries a 1⁻ charge.*

The noble gases

The noble gases are very **unreactive**. They are sometimes described as being 'inert' because they do not react. This is because they have a full, **stable** outer shell of electrons.

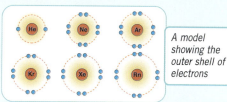

A model showing the outer shell of electrons

Characteristics of noble gases

- The noble gases are found on the far right-hand side of the periodic table.
- The noble gases are all colourless.
- They are **monatomic gases** – this means that they exist as single atoms rather than as **diatomic** molecules as other gases do.

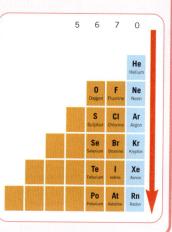

Why are noble gases so unreactive?

When atoms react they share, gain or lose electrons to obtain a full outer shell. **Noble gases already have a full and stable outer shell so they do not react.** Noble gases are useful precisely because they do not react, however.

Uses of the noble gases

Helium
- Helium is used in balloons and in airships.
- It is less dense than air.
- It is not flammable. (Early airships used hydrogen which is flammable and this caused problems.)

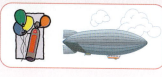

Neon
- Neon is used in electrical discharge tubes in advertising signs.

Argon
- Argon is used in filament light bulbs.
- The hot filament is surrounded by argon. This stops the filament from burning away which would break the bulb.

Krypton
- Krypton is used in lasers.

KEY TERMS

Make sure you understand these terms before moving on!
- ionic compounds
- unreactive
- stable
- monatomic
- diatomic

QUICK TEST

1. What is the name used for Group 7?
2. What is the trend in reactivity down Group 7?
3. What is helium used for?
4. Why is it used?
5. What is neon used for?
6. What is argon used for?
7. What is krypton used for?

Making salts

Salts are very important materials. Uses of salts include:

- the production of fertilisers
- fireworks

Making salts from metal carbonates

Metal carbonates can be neutralised by acids to form salts. Most metal carbonates are insoluble, so they are **bases**, but they are not **alkalis**. When metal carbonates are **neutralised**, salts, water and carbon dioxide are produced.

The general equation for the reaction is:

metal carbonate + acid ➡ salt + water + carbon dioxide

Examples

zinc carbonate + sulphuric acid ➡ zinc sulphate + water + carbon dioxide

copper carbonate + hydrochloric acid ➡ copper chloride + water + carbon dioxide

This diagram shows how copper chloride salt is made.

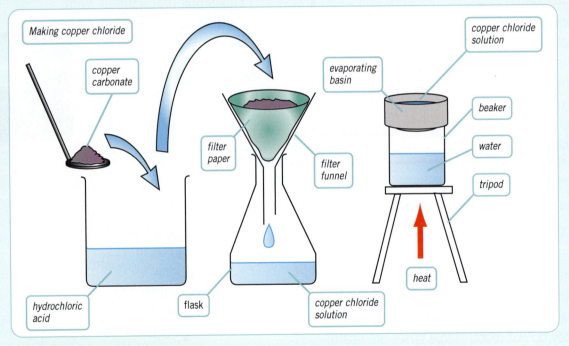

Making copper chloride

copper carbonate

filter paper

filter funnel

evaporating basin

copper chloride solution

beaker

water

tripod

heat

hydrochloric acid

flask

copper chloride solution

The steps involved in the production of copper chloride are:

- Copper carbonate is added to hydrochloric acid until all the acid is used up.
- Any unreacted copper carbonate is **filtered off**.
- The solution of copper chloride and water is poured into an evaporating basin.
- The basin is **heated gently** until the first crystals of copper chloride start to appear.
- The solution is then left on a warm windowsill or near a radiator for a few days to allow the remaining copper chloride to **crystallise**.

- *Sulphuric acid is neutralised to form sulphate salts.*
- *Hydrochloric acid is neutralised to form chloride salts.*
- *Nitric acid is neutralised to form nitrate salts.*

Metal hydroxides

Metal hydroxides can be reacted with acids to form a salt and water.

Salts of very reactive metals like sodium can be made in this way.

Examples

> sodium hydroxide + hydrochloric acid ➡ sodium chloride + water
> magnesium + sulphuric acid ➡ magnesium sulphate + water

Metal oxides

Metal oxides are also bases: they can be reacted with acids to make salts and water:

> metal oxide + acid ➡ salt + water

Examples

> copper oxide + hydrochloric acid ➡ copper chloride + water
> zinc oxide + sulphuric acid ➡ zinc sulphate + water

Precipitation reactions

Some **insoluble** salts can be made from the reaction between two solutions.

Barium sulphate is an insoluble salt. It can be made by the reaction between solutions of barium chloride and sodium sulphate:

> barium chloride + sodium sulphate ➡ barium sulphate + sodium chloride

The insoluble barium sulphate can be filtered off, washed and dried. Overall, the two original salts, barium chloride and sodium sulphate, have swapped partners. This can be described as a double decomposition reaction.

The chloride ions and sodium ions are **spectator ions**. They are present but they are not involved in the reaction.

KEY TERMS

Make sure you understand these terms before moving on!
- base
- alkali
- neutralised
- crystallise
- insoluble

QUICK TEST

1. What is formed when hydrochloric acid reacts with potassium hydroxide?

2. What is formed when sulphuric acid reacts with sodium hydroxide?

3. What gas is given off when metal carbonates react with acids?

4. What is formed when hydrochloric acid reacts with zinc carbonate?

5. What is formed when sulphuric acid reacts with magnesium carbonate?

6. How could you get a sample of a soluble salt from a salt solution?

7. What is formed when hydrochloric acid reacts with magnesium?

8. What is formed when sulphuric acid reacts with zinc?

9. What is formed when hydrochloric acid reacts with zinc oxide?

10. What is formed when sulphuric acid reacts with copper oxide?

Limestone

What is limestone?

Limestone is a sedimentary rock. It is mainly composed of the chemical calcium carbonate. It can be **quarried** and cut into blocks, which can be used for building.

> Rocks can be classified into three groups; sedimentary, metamorphic and igneous. Marble is an example of a metamorphic rock. Marble is made when limestone is subjected to high pressures and temperatures. Granite is an example of an igneous rock. Igneous rocks are harder than metamorphic rocks which are harder than sedimentary rocks.

If limestone is powdered it can be used to neutralise the acidity in lakes caused by acid rain and to neutralise acidic soils.

> The thermal decomposition of limestone is an example of a reaction which takes in heat. This is called an endothermic reaction.

Heating limestone

When **limestone** (calcium carbonate) is heated, it breaks down to form **quicklime** (calcium oxide) and **carbon dioxide**:

> calcium carbonate ➡ calcium oxide + carbon dioxide

This is an example of a **thermal decomposition** reaction.

Quicklime (calcium oxide) can be reacted with water to form **slaked lime** (**calcium hydroxide**). This reaction gives out energy and is an example of an **exothermic reaction**.

A solution of slaked lime is known as limewater:

> calcium oxide + water ➡ calcium hydroxide

Calcium oxide and calcium hydroxide are both **bases** so they can be used to neutralise acidic lakes and soils.

> The formula $CaCO_3$ shows us the type and ratio of atoms present. Here the calcium, carbon and oxygen atoms are present in the ratio 1 : 1 : 3.

> Calcium oxide is an example of a compound which is held together by ionic bonds. Ionic bonding involves the transfer of electrons. This forms ions with opposite charges which then attract each other.

Reaction summary

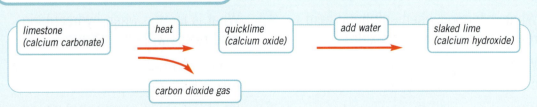

Similar thermal decomposition reactions

Other metal carbonates decompose in a **similar way** when they are heated.

When copper carbonate is heated it breaks down to give copper oxide and carbon dioxide:

> copper carbonate ➡ copper oxide + carbon dioxide

Other uses of limestone

Limestone can be used to make other useful materials, including glass, cement and concrete.

Heating baking powder

When **metal hydrogen carbonate compounds** are heated they undergo thermal decomposition reactions to form **metal carbonates, carbon dioxide and water**.

The main chemical compound in baking powder is sodium hydrogen carbonate, $NaHCO_3$.
When heated fiercely it reacts to form sodium carbonate, carbon dioxide and water:

sodium hydrogen carbonate ➡ sodium carbonate + carbon dioxide + water

KEY TERMS

Make sure you understand these terms before moving on!

- quarried
- quicklime
- thermal decomposition
- slaked lime

QUICK TEST

1. What is the main chemical in limestone?

2. What type of rock is limestone?

3. What type of rock is granite?

4. What is powdered limestone used for?

5. Give the word equation for the thermal decomposition of calcium carbonate.

6. Give the word equation for the thermal decomposition of zinc carbonate.

7. Name the three products formed by the thermal decomposition of sodium hydrogen carbonate.

Fuels

Fuels are burnt to release energy. In this country the fossil fuels coal, oil and gas are widely used.

Formation of coal, oil and gas

Fossil fuels are formed over **millions of years** from the fossilised remains of dead plants and animals. When these plants and animals died, they fell to the sea or swamp floor. Occasionally, the remains were covered by sediment very quickly. In the absence of oxygen, the remains did not decay. Over time, more layers of sediment gradually built up. The lower layers became heated and pressurised. Over millions of years, fossil fuels formed. Fossil fuels are non-renewable. They take millions of years to form, but are being used up very quickly.

 Coal is mainly carbon. Petrol, diesel and oil are hydrocarbons.

Crude oil

Crude oil, like many natural substances, is a **mixture**. In fact, crude oil is a mixture of many substances, but the most important are called **hydrocarbons**. Hydrocarbons are molecules that only contain carbon and hydrogen atoms. When hydrocarbons are burnt in oxygen, carbon dioxide, water and energy are released.

Some of the hydrocarbons have very short chains of carbon atoms. These hydrocarbons:

■ are runny
■ are easy to **ignite**
■ have low boiling points
■ are valuable fuels.

Other hydrocarbon molecules have much longer chains of carbon atoms.

These hydrocarbon molecules:

■ are more **viscous** (less runny)
■ are harder to ignite
■ have higher boiling points.

These longer hydrocarbon molecules are less useful as fuels. Before any of these hydrocarbon molecules can be used, however, they must first be separated into groups of molecules with a similar number of carbon atoms called **fractions**.

 In compounds, the atoms of two or more different elements are chemically combined. In mixtures, two or more different elements or compounds are simply mixed together. Each constituent part of the mixture has its original chemical properties. This makes it quite easy to separate mixtures.

Fractional distillation of crude oil

Crude oil can be separated by **fractional distillation**. First, the crude oil is heated until it eventually evaporates. The diagram of the fractionating column shows that the bottom of the fractionating column is much hotter than the top of the column. This means that short hydrocarbon molecules can reach the top of the column before they condense and are collected. Longer hydrocarbon molecules condense at higher temperatures and are collected at different points down the column.

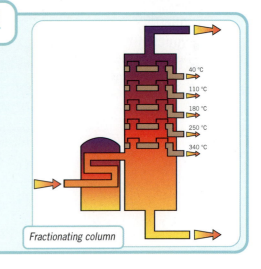

Fractionating column

Cracking

The large hydrocarbon molecules separated during the fractional distillation of crude oil are not very useful. These hydrocarbon molecules can, however, be broken down into smaller, more useful and more valuable molecules by a process called **cracking**.

Cracking large hydrocarbon molecules can produce more useful products. Some of these molecules are used as fuels

Industrial cracking

- The cracking of long-chain hydrocarbons is carried out on a large scale.
- First, the long hydrocarbon molecules are heated until they evaporate.
- The vapour is then passed over a catalyst.
- In this example, decane is being cracked to produce octane and ethene.

decane $C_{10}H_{22}$ (from the naphtha fraction) $\longrightarrow$ octane C_8H_{18} + ethene C_2H_4

$$H-\overset{\displaystyle H}{\underset{\displaystyle H}{C}}-\overset{\displaystyle H}{\underset{\displaystyle H}{C}}-\overset{\displaystyle H}{\underset{\displaystyle H}{C}}-\overset{\displaystyle H}{\underset{\displaystyle H}{C}}-\overset{\displaystyle H}{\underset{\displaystyle H}{C}}-\overset{\displaystyle H}{\underset{\displaystyle H}{C}}-\overset{\displaystyle H}{\underset{\displaystyle H}{C}}-\overset{\displaystyle H}{\underset{\displaystyle H}{C}}-\overset{\displaystyle H}{\underset{\displaystyle H}{C}}-\overset{\displaystyle H}{\underset{\displaystyle H}{C}}-H$$

Octane is one of the hydrocarbon molecules in petrol. **Ethene**, which is a member of the **alkene family** of hydrocarbons, is also produced. Ethene is used to make a range of new compounds including plastics and industrial alcohol.

💡 *Cracking is an example of a thermal decomposition reaction. Some of the products of the cracking are very useful fuels.*

QUICK TEST

1. Name three fossil fuels.
2. How long does it take for fossil fuels to form?
3. Which elements are found in hydrocarbon molecules?
4. Give three properties of short-chain hydrocarbon molecules.
5. Which hydrocarbons make the best fuels?
6. Where are the short-chain hydrocarbon molecules collected in a fractionating column?
7. Why are long-chain hydrocarbons cracked to form smaller ones?
8. What family does ethene belong to?
9. What does a 'fraction' mean in this context?

Sodium chloride

Sodium chloride

Sodium chloride (common salt) is an important resource. Sodium chloride is dissolved in large quantities in seawater. It is also found in vast underground deposits which formed as ancient seas evaporated.

Rock salt (unpurified salt) is often used on icy roads. The salt lowers the freezing point of water from 0 °C to about –5 °C. Sprinkling rock salt on roads means that any water present will not freeze to form ice unless the temperature is very low.

A solution of sodium chloride in water is called **brine**.

Electrolysis

The **electrolysis** of concentrated sodium chloride solution is an important industrial process.

During electrolysis, the ions move towards the oppositely charged electrode. The electrolysis of sodium chloride solution produces three useful products:

- During electrolysis, pairs of hydrogen H^+ ions are attracted to the negative electrode where they pick up electrons to form **hydrogen molecules** H_2:

hydrogen ions + electrons ➡ hydrogen molecules

- Pairs of chloride Cl^- ions are attracted to the positive electrode where they deposit electrons to form **chlorine molecules**:

chloride ions − electrons ➡ chlorine molecules

- A solution of **sodium hydroxide** NaOH is also produced.

Each of these products can be used to make other useful materials.

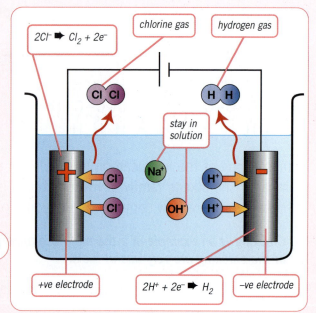

$2Cl^- ➡ Cl_2 + 2e^-$

chlorine gas

hydrogen gas

stay in solution

+ve electrode

$2H^+ + 2e^- ➡ H_2$

−ve electrode

Oxidation and reduction

In the electrolysis of concentrated sodium chloride solution:

- **Hydrogen ions are reduced to hydrogen molecules.**
- **Chloride ions are oxidised to chlorine molecules.**

Reduction reactions happen when a substance gains **electrons**. Here, two hydrogen ions both gain an electron to form a hydrogen molecule.

Oxidation reactions occur when a substance loses electrons. Here, two chloride ions both lose an electron to form a chlorine molecule.

Reduction and oxidation reactions must always occur together and so are sometimes referred to as **redox** reactions.

Useful products from the electrolysis of sodium chloride solution

Chlorine

This is used:

- to make bleach
- **to sterilise water**
- to produce hydrochloric acid
- in the production of PVC.

Hydrogen

Hydrogen is used in the manufacture of margarine.

Sodium hydroxide

This is an alkali used in paper-making and in the manufacture of many products including:

- soaps and detergents
- rayon and acetate fibres.

Electrolysis of molten sodium chloride

Solid sodium chloride does not conduct electricity because the ions cannot move. If, however, sodium chloride is heated until it becomes molten, the **sodium ions and chloride ions can then move.**

During the electrolysis of molten sodium chloride, the ions move **towards the oppositely charged electrodes.** Sodium Na^+ ions are attracted to the **negative electrode** where they pick up electrons to form sodium Na atoms:

sodium ion + electron ➡ sodium atom

Pairs of chloride ions Cl^- ions are attracted to the **positive electrode** where they deposit electrons to form chlorine molecules:

chloride ions − electrons ➡ chlorine molecules

KEY TERMS

Make sure you understand these terms before moving on!

- electrolysis
- reduction
- electrons
- oxidation
- negative electrode
- positive electrode

QUICK TEST

1. What groups do sodium and chlorine belong to?
2. Where is sodium chloride found?
3. Why are roads 'salted'?
4. What is brine?
5. During the electrolysis of brine, what is produced at the positive electrode?
6. During the electrolysis of brine, what is produced at the negative electrode?
7. Which other useful chemical is produced?
8. How is chlorine used?
9. How is hydrogen used?
10. How is sodium hydroxide used?

Vegetable oils

Plant oils are a valuable source of energy in our diets. They are also essential sources of vitamins A and D. However, if we eat too many vegetable oils we could suffer from health problems, such as heart disease, in later life.

Vegetable oils can be produced from the fruits, seeds or nuts of some plants. Popular vegetable oils include olive oil and sunflower oil.

Using fats for cooking

Fats have **higher boiling points** than water. Cooking food by frying is therefore much faster than cooking food by boiling. Frying also produces interesting **new flavours** and **increases the energy content** of the food.

Chips are made by frying potatoes

Fuels

When vegetable oils are burnt, they release lots of energy. In fact, vegetable oils can be used in place of fossil fuels in the production of **bio-diesel**. This is an alternative to normal diesel which is produced from the fossil fuel crude oil.

What is a fat molecule?

Fats and oils are complex molecules.

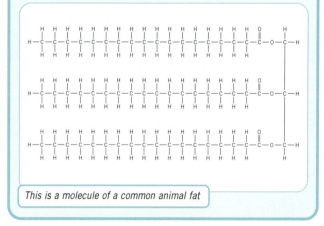

This is a molecule of a common animal fat

Emulsions

Salad dressing is an example of a type of everyday mixture called an **emulsion**. Salad dressing is a **mixture of two liquids**: oil and vinegar. It is made by shaking the oil and vinegar together so that they mix. After a short while, however, the oil and vinegar **separate out to form two distinct layers**. Many of the salad dressings bought from shops contain molecules called emulsifiers, which help the oil and vinegar to mix together. Emulsifiers are molecules which have two very different ends. One end is attracted to oil (hydrophobic), while the other end is attracted to the water in the vinegar (hydrophilic). The addition of emulsifiers keeps the two liquids mixed together.

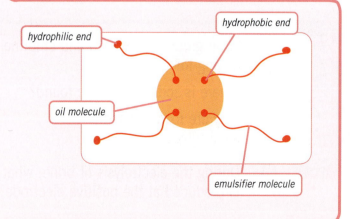

hydrophilic end

hydrophobic end

oil molecule

emulsifier molecule

Food additives

Scientists often add chemicals to foods to improve it. Many modern convenience foods contain additives. The chemicals that have passed safety tests and are approved for use throughout the European Union are called **E-numbers**. Chemicals that are added to foods include:

- **Emulsifiers** – which help ingredients to mix together.
- **Colours** – which are added to food to make it look more attractive.
- **Flavours** – which are added to enhance taste.
- **Artificial sweeteners** – which are used to decrease the amount of sugar used.

Scientists can identify the additives present in foods by chemical analysis. Artificial colours can be detected using chromotography.

Are all food additives bad for you?

Substances, like salt, have been added to food for thousands of years. A lack of iodine in the diet can cause severe mental retardation. Iodine can be added to salt in small amounts and this can protect people from developing problems. There are clearly some health benefits to adding some substances to food.

Do artificial ingredients cause health problems?

Artificial ingredients are not found in nature. They are manufactured by people. While any substance can be harmful in excessive amounts, provided we eat a variety of foods to ensure that we never eat too much of any particular additive, scientists believe that permitted additives are safe.

Natural substances are not necessarily safe and artificial substances are not necessarily unsafe. Arsenic is a natural substance that is extremely toxic.

KEY TERMS

Make sure you understand these terms before moving on!
- energy
- bio-diesel
- emulsion
- E-numbers
- artificial ingredients

QUICK TEST

1. Which parts of plants can we obtain oils from?
2. Which part of a sunflower is used to obtain oil?
3. Which vitamins do we obtain from eating fats?
4. Why is frying food faster than boiling food?
5. Will a food that has been fried or boiled contain more energy?
6. What is an 'E-number'?
7. Why are artificial colours used?
8. Why are emulsifiers added to foods?
9. Why are artificial sweeteners added to foods?
10. Are all natural additives safe?

Ethanol

Ethanol is a member of the *alcohol* family of organic compounds.

Uses of ethanol

Ethanol has the structure:

```
      H   H
      |   |
  H — C — C — O — H
      |   |
      H   H
```

It is found in drinks like beer and wine. It is, however, toxic in large amounts. Ethanol has many useful properties. It is a **good solvent** and evaporates quickly. Many aftershaves contain ethanol. Ethanol is an important raw material and can also be used as a **fuel.**

Methanol is another member of the alcohol group. Methanol is even more toxic than ethanol. If someone were to drink methanol they could become blind or even die. Methylated spirit is a mixture of ethanol, methanol plus a purple dye. The purple dye is to warn people that it is toxic and its very unpleasant taste is to try and stop people from drinking it.

Ethanol as a fuel

In some countries sugar beet or sugar cane is made into alcohol. This alcohol can then be mixed with petrol to produce a fuel for vehicles like cars. Ethanol is a **renewable energy** resource which burns very cleanly. However, **alcohols release less energy** than petrol when they are burnt. Also, in order to produce the plants needed to manufacture the alcohol large areas of fertile land are required.

Sugar cane can be used to produce alcohol which can be burnt as a fuel

Fermentation 1

Fermentation has been used to make alcohol for thousands of years. We use fermentation to make alcoholic drinks. Fruits, vegetables and cereals are all sources of the sugar **glucose**, $C_6H_{12}O_6$.

During fermentation, **yeast** is used to catalyse (speed up) the reaction in which glucose is converted into ethanol and carbon dioxide.

$$\text{glucose} \xrightarrow{\text{yeast}} \text{ethanol} + \text{carbon dioxide}$$

The temperature of the reaction has to be carefully controlled. If the temperature falls too low, the yeast stops working as fast and the rate of the reaction slows down. If the temperature rises too high, the yeast is denatured and stops working altogether.

Fermentation 2

Ethanol produced by fermentation has a concentration of around 6 to 14%. Some people prefer drinks with a higher alcohol content. These higher concentrations are achieved by **fractional distillation**. There is a very strong link, however, between the consumption of alcohol and an increased risk of accidents and raised levels of crime. Some religions prohibit the consumption of all alcoholic drinks altogether.

 Yeast is an enzyme or biological catalyst. It speeds up the conversion of sugar to alcohol and carbon dioxide but is not itself used up.

The fermentation lock allows carbon dioxide to escape, but stops oxygen in the air from reaching the alcohol. This is important as ethanol can be easily oxidised to ethanoic acid, which would make the drink taste sour

Industrial alcohol

There is another, more modern way of producing vast amounts of alcohol.

In this method, **ethene** (which is produced during the cracking of long-chain hydrocarbons) is **reacted with steam to produce ethanol**:

ethene + steam ➡ ethanol

A catalyst of **phosphoric acid and a temperature of 300 °C** are used.

This method of producing ethanol is much cheaper than fermentation.

KEY TERMS

Make sure you understand these terms before moving on!

- alcohol
- solvent
- renewable
- fermentation
- glucose
- yeast

QUICK TEST

1. What is the formula of ethanol?
2. Give three uses of ethanol.
3. What could happen to someone who drinks the alcohol methanol?
4. What is added to methylated spirit to stop people from drinking it?
5. What is the name of the alcohol mixture used as a fuel in some countries?
6. What is the catalyst used in fermentation?
7. What is the formula of glucose?
8. What happens to yeast if the temperature is too high?
9. What is the name of the catalyst that is used in the industrial production of ethanol?
10. What is the word equation for the industrial production of ethanol?

Evolution of the atmosphere

The *composition* of today's atmosphere is:

- about 80% nitrogen
- about 20% oxygen
- small amounts of other gases such as carbon dioxide, water vapour and noble gases, e.g. argon.

The atmosphere's composition has remained stable for the last 200 million years. This has not always been the case. Over the history of the Earth, the composition of the atmosphere has changed and evolved.

Formation of the atmosphere

The first billion years
- During the first billion years of the Earth's life, there was **enormous volcanic activity**.
- The volcanoes belched out carbon dioxide (CO_2), steam (H_2O), ammonia (NH_3) and methane (CH_4).
- The atmosphere was **mainly carbon dioxide** and there was very little oxygen. In fact, Earth's early atmosphere was very similar to the modern-day atmospheres of the planets **Mars and Venus**.
- The steam condensed to form the early oceans.

Later
- During the next two billion years, **plants evolved** and began to cover the surface of the Earth.
- The plants grew very well in the carbon dioxide-rich atmosphere and steadily removed carbon dioxide and produced oxygen (O_2).

Later still
- Most of the carbon from the carbon dioxide in the early atmosphere gradually became **locked up** as carbonate minerals and fossil fuels in sedimentary rocks.
- The ammonia in the early atmosphere reacted with oxygen to release nitrogen.
- Nitrogen was also produced by living organisms such as denitrifying bacteria.
- As the amount of oxygen increased, an **ozone** layer (O_3) developed. This layer filtered out harmful ultraviolet radiation from the Sun. This enabled new, more complex life forms to develop.

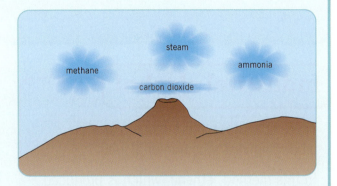

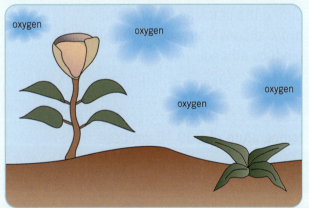

This limestone rock is rich in the chemical calcium carbonate

Is burning fossil fuels going to cause problems?

The level of carbon dioxide in our atmosphere has increased since the Industrial Revolution as we have burnt more fossil fuels. These fossil fuels had stored carbon dioxide from the Earth's early atmosphere for hundreds of millions of years.

There is a mismatch, however, between the amount of carbon dioxide released into the atmosphere by the burning of fossil fuels and the actual increase in the amount of carbon dioxide in the atmosphere. A lot of the carbon dioxide appears to be missing. Scientists believe that much of the carbon dioxide that is produced is removed from the atmosphere by the

reaction between carbon dioxide and seawater. This reaction produces:

- **insoluble carbonate** salts which are deposited as sediment
- **soluble calcium and magnesium hydrogen carbonate** salts, which sometimes end up as sediment.

Much of the carbon dioxide is therefore locked up in sediment for long periods of time. Some of this carbon dioxide is later released back into the atmosphere when the sediment is subducted underground by geological activity and then becomes involved in volcanoes.

Not all of the carbon dioxide released by the burning of fossil fuels, however, is removed in these ways. Many people are concerned about rising levels of carbon dioxide in the Earth's atmosphere and the possible link between these increased levels and **global warming**.

Scientific process

Our ideas about the **evolution** of the Earth's atmosphere have come from scientists' studies of rocks formed in the past. Our ideas have changed as more evidence has become available. Today we use computer models to project what might happen in the future. These projections, however, are not always correct.

KEY TERMS

Make sure you understand these terms before moving on!
- composition
- formation
- volcanic activity
- ozone
- global warming
- evolution

QUICK TEST

1. Roughly how much of today's atmosphere is made up of oxygen?

2. What is the main gas in the atmosphere today?

3. What other gases are present in small amounts in the Earth's atmosphere?

4. Which gases formed the Earth's early atmosphere?

5. Which was the main gas in the Earth's early atmosphere?

6. How did the evolution of plants affect the Earth's atmosphere?

7. What happened to most of the carbon dioxide in the Earth's early atmosphere?

8. What does the ozone layer do?

9. How did the development of the ozone layer affect life on Earth?

10. Why is the amount of carbon dioxide in the Earth's atmosphere increasing?

Pollution of the atmosphere

The atmosphere can be polluted in many ways.

Acid rain

Fossil fuels like coal, oil and gas often contain small amounts of **sulphur**. When these fuels are burnt, the gas **sulphur dioxide**, SO_2, is produced. This gas can dissolve in rain water to form **acid rain**. Acid rain can affect the environment by damaging statues and buildings as well as plants and animals that live in water.

Carbon monoxide

The gas **carbon monoxide**, CO, can also cause problems.

- When fossil fuels which contain carbon and hydrogen are burnt the gases carbon dioxide and water vapour are produced.
- However, if carbon is burnt in a poor **supply of oxygen,** the gas carbon monoxide can also be produced.
- Carbon monoxide is colourless, odourless and very poisonous. Carbon monoxide molecules can bond to red blood cells and this reduces the amount of oxygen that these blood cells can carry around the body.
- Faulty gas appliances can produce carbon monoxide so it is important that they are regularly serviced.

Incomplete combustion is undesirable because:

- *carbon monoxide is produced*
- *less heat than expected is given off when the fuel is burnt*
- *soot is produced, which must then be cleaned. A sooty flame has a yellow colour.*

Global dimming

Global dimming is caused by sooty **smoke particles** that are released into the atmosphere. Scientists believe that these smoke particles reduce the amount of sunlight that reaches the Earth's surface and may even affect weather patterns.

Carbon dioxide and the greenhouse effect

The **greenhouse effect** is slowly heating up the Earth.

- When fossil fuels are burnt, the gas carbon dioxide is produced.
- Although some of this carbon dioxide is removed from the atmosphere by the reaction between carbon dioxide and seawater, the overall amount of carbon dioxide in the atmosphere has increased over the last two hundred years.
- The carbon dioxide gas **traps the heat energy** that has reached the Earth from the Sun.

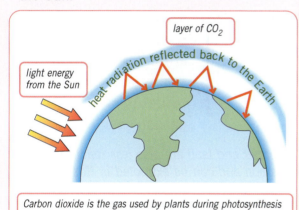

layer of CO_2

light energy from the Sun

heat radiation reflected back to the Earth

Carbon dioxide is the gas used by plants during photosynthesis

- Global warming may mean that the polar icecaps will eventually melt and this could cause massive flooding.

🛈 *Carbon dioxide is the gas used by plants during photosynthesis.*

Scientific theory

Not all scientists believe that human activity is causing global warming. Other factors such as solar cycles may be more important. Until we have more evidence, we will not really know.

Problems with bauxite quarrying

Aluminium is extracted from its ore **bauxite**. Unfortunately, this ore is often found in environmentally sensitive areas like the Amazonian **rainforest.** Bauxite is extracted from large open-cast mines. Every new mine means that many trees have to be cut down. Trees also have to be cleared when new roads are built to give access to the mines. In addition, the area around the mine can be polluted by litter and oil.

Aluminium can be recycled, however. This cuts down on landfill in this country and helps to preserve the rainforests.

KEY TERMS

Make sure you understand these terms before moving on!
- acid rain
- carbon monoxide
- global dimming
- greenhouse effect

QUICK TEST

1. What is the name of the gas produced when sulphur is burnt?
2. Which fossil fuel contains the most sulphur?
3. How can switching off lights prevent the formation of acid rain?
4. How can you tell if a fuel is being burnt in a poor supply of oxygen?
5. What gas is produced when carbon is burnt in a good supply of oxygen?
6. What gas is produced when carbon is burnt in an insufficient supply of oxygen?
7. What causes global dimming?
8. What are the problems associated with global dimming?

Extraction of iron

Iron is an element. Elements are substances which are made of only one type of atom. There are only about one hundred different elements.

Iron is an extremely important metal. It is extracted from iron ore in a blast furnace.

Methods of extraction

The more reactive a metal is, the harder it is to remove it from its compound.

Gold, for instance, is so unreactive that it is found uncombined. All other metals, however, are found in compounds. Occasionally we may find rocks that contain metals in such high concentrations that it is economically worthwhile to **extract** the metal from the rock. Such rocks are called **ores**.

The exact method chosen to extract the metal depends on the reactivity of the metal.

Iron is less reactive than carbon. Iron can be extracted from iron oxide by reducing the metal oxide with carbon. **Reduction** is the loss of oxygen from a substance.

potassium
sodium
calcium
magnesium
aluminium
} Metals that are more reactive than carbon are extracted by *electrolysis*.

carbon

zinc
iron
tin
lead
gold
} Metals that are less reactive than carbon are extracted by reducing the metal oxide using *carbon* (or carbon monoxide).

Copper and lead are also less reactive than carbon and can be extracted in this way.

The solid raw materials

The solid raw materials in the blast furnace are:

- iron ore
- **coke** (which is a source of the element carbon)

- **limestone** (which reacts with impurities).

The main ore of iron is **haematite**. This ore contains the compound iron (III) oxide, Fe_2O_3.

What happens in the blast furnace 1

1 First, hot air is blasted into the furnace. The oxygen in the air reacts with the carbon in the coke to form carbon dioxide and release energy:

carbon + oxygen ➡ carbon dioxide

2 At the very high temperatures inside the blast furnace carbon dioxide reacts with more carbon to form carbon monoxide:

carbon dioxide + carbon ➡ carbon monoxide

3 The carbon monoxide reacts with iron oxide to form iron and carbon dioxide:

carbon monoxide + iron oxide ➡ iron + carbon dioxide

What happens in the blast furnace 2

During this reaction:

- the iron oxide is reduced to iron
- the carbon monoxide is oxidised to carbon dioxide.

4 Due to the high temperatures in the blast furnace, the iron that is made is a liquid. This molten iron is dense and sinks to the bottom of the furnace where it can be removed.

ⓘ *Iron ore is mainly reduced by the gas carbon monoxide.*

Removing impurities in the blast furnace

Haematite (iron ore) contains many impurities. Most commonly, it contains substantial amounts of silicon dioxide (silica). Limestone is added to the blast furnace because it reacts with these silica impurities to form **slag**. Slag has a low **density** so floats to the top of the iron ore where it can be removed. The slag can be used in road building and in the manufacture of fertilisers.

ⓘ *Oxidation is the addition of oxygen to a substance.*

ⓘ *Reduction is the removal of oxygen from a substance.*

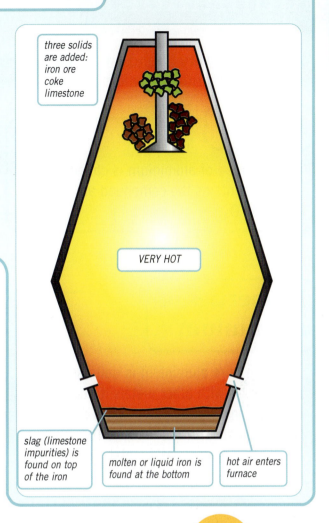

three solids are added:
iron ore
coke
limestone

VERY HOT

slag (limestone impurities) is found on top of the iron

molten or liquid iron is found at the bottom

hot air enters furnace

KEY TERMS

Make sure you understand these terms before moving on!

- extraction
- ore
- reduction
- coke
- limestone
- density

QUICK TEST

1 Which element is so unreactive that it can be found uncombined?

2 Which method of extraction can be used for metals that are less reactive than carbon?

3 Which method of extraction can be used for metals that are more reactive than carbon?

4 What is the name of the main ore of iron?

5 What are the three solid raw materials added to the blast furnace?

6 What is the other raw material used in the blast furnace?

7 Which gas mainly reduces iron oxide to iron?

Aluminium

Aluminium is very abundant in the Earth's crust but it is also very reactive. Consequently, aluminium is more expensive than iron.

Bauxite

The main **ore** of aluminium is called **bauxite**. Bauxite contains the compound aluminium oxide, Al_2O_3.

Properties of aluminium

Although pure aluminium is quite soft, when it is alloyed with other metals it becomes much stronger. **Aluminium alloys combine high strength with low density**. This makes aluminium a very useful metal for making objects like aeroplanes and mountain bikes.

Aluminium is quite a reactive metal and yet it is widely used to make drinks cans. In fact, aluminium appears to be much less reactive than its position in the reactivity series suggests. This is because, when aluminium objects are made, their surfaces quickly react with oxygen to form a thin **layer of aluminium oxide**. This layer stops the aluminium metal from coming into contact with other

Recycling aluminium

One way to protect the areas where bauxite is found is for people to simply **recycle** their old aluminium cans. Recycling has many advantages:

- We will not have to extract so much bauxite.
- Landfill sites are not filled up with discarded aluminium cans.
- Recycling aluminium uses much less energy than extracting aluminium straight from its ore.

chemicals and so prevents any further reaction. This layer of aluminium oxide means that it is quite safe for us to drink fizzy, acidic drinks from aluminium cans.

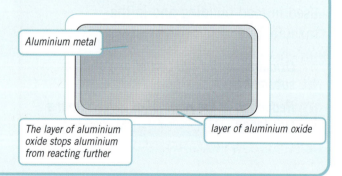

Aluminium metal

The layer of aluminium oxide stops aluminium from reacting further

layer of aluminium oxide

The extraction of aluminium

Aluminium is more reactive than carbon so it is **extracted** using electrolysis, even though this is a very expensive method. The main ore of aluminium is bauxite, which contains aluminium oxide. For electrolysis to occur, the aluminium ions and oxide ions in bauxite must be able to move. This means that the bauxite has to be either heated until it melts or dissolved in something.

Bauxite has a very high melting point and heating the ore to this temperature would be very expensive. Fortunately, we have found that another ore of aluminium called **cryolite** has a much lower melting point. First, the cryolite is heated up until it melts and then the bauxite is **dissolved** in the molten cryolite.

Electrolysis

Aluminium can now be extracted by electrolysis.

1 By dissolving the aluminium oxide both the aluminium Al^{3+} and the oxide O^{2-} ions can move.

2 During electrolysis, the aluminium Al^{3+} ions are attracted to the negative electrode where they pick up electrons to form aluminium Al atoms. The aluminium metal collects at the bottom of the cell.

> aluminium ions + electrons ➡ aluminium atoms

3 The oxide O^{2-} ions are attracted to the positive electrode where they deposit electrons to form oxygen molecules.

> oxide ions − electrons ➡ oxygen molecules

4 The oxygen that forms at the positive electrode readily reacts with the **carbon, graphite electrode** to form carbon dioxide. So the electrodes must be replaced periodically.

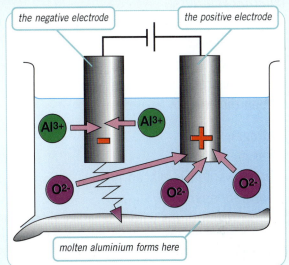

the negative electrode

the positive electrode

molten aluminium forms here

Oxidation and reduction

In the electrolysis of aluminium oxide:

- **aluminium ions are reduced to aluminium atoms**
- **oxide ions are oxidised to oxygen molecules.**

Reduction and oxidation reactions must always occur together and so are sometimes referred to as **redox** reactions.

KEY TERMS

Make sure you understand these terms before moving on!

- ore
- bauxite
- recycling
- density
- extraction
- cryolite
- oxidation
- reduction

QUICK TEST

1 Name the main ore of aluminium.

2 Give two properties of pure aluminium.

3 What is a mixture of metals called?

4 Why is aluminium less reactive than expected?

5 What is the formula of aluminium oxide?

6 What is the name of the method used to extract aluminium from its ore?

7 During the electrolysis of aluminium oxide which ions are oxidised?

8 During the electrolysis of aluminium oxide which ions are reduced?

9 What are the electrodes made from?

10 Why should the electrodes be periodically replaced?

Chemical tests

In this subject, we often wish to *identify* the chemical present.

Gas tests

Carbon dioxide
What do you do?
The gas is bubbled through **limewater**.
What happens?
The limewater turns cloudy.
Carbonates react with acids to produce
carbon dioxide.

Hydrogen
What do you do?
A lighted splint is placed nearby.
What happens?
The hydrogen burns with a squeaky pop.

Chlorine
What do you do?
Place damp litmus paper in the gas.
What happens?
The litmus paper is **bleached**.

Oxygen
What do you do?
A glowing splint is placed in the gas.
What happens?
The splint relights.

Ammonia
What do you do?
Place damp red litmus paper in the gas.
What happens?
The red litmus paper turns blue.

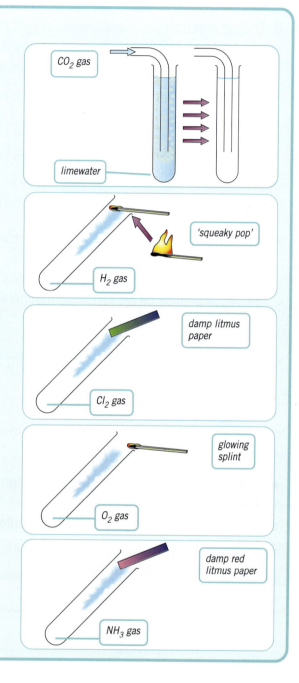

Flame tests

Flame tests can be used to identify some metals present in salts.

What do you do?
- Clean a flame test wire by placing it into the hottest part of a Bunsen flame.
- Dip the end of the wire into water and then into the salt sample.

- Hold the sample in the hottest part of the flame and observe the colour seen.

What happens?
- lithium ⟶ red
- sodium ⟶ orange
- potassium ⟶ lilac
- calcium ⟶ brick red
- barium ⟶ apple green

Hazard symbols

The containers of some chemicals show hazard symbols. The symbols alert users to the potential hazards of using the chemicals.

Oxidising
Provides oxygen which allows other materials to burn more fiercely.

Highly flammable
Catches fire very easily.

Toxic
Can cause death if swallowed, breathed in or absorbed through the skin.

Harmful
Similar to toxic, but less dangerous.

Corrosive
Attacks and destroys living tissues, including eyes and skin.

Irritant
Not corrosive but can cause reddening or blistering of the skin.

Hydroxide tests

We can identify other metals by adding sodium hydroxide solution to solutions of the salt. If the unknown metal forms an **insoluble precipitate**, we can use the colour of the precipitate to identify the metal present:

- copper (II) – pale blue precipitate
- iron (II) – green precipitate
- iron (III) – brown precipitate

Modern instrumental methods

Modern instrumental techniques can be used to **detect and identify chemicals**. These modern techniques have many advantages in that they are:

- accurate
- sensitive
- fast
- can be used when there are only very small samples available.

These techniques can be very useful to forensic scientists who are identifying substances found at crime scenes.

KEY TERMS

Make sure you understand these terms before moving on!
- identify
- limewater
- bleached
- insoluble precipitate

QUICK TEST

1. What is the test for carbon dioxide?
2. What is the test for chlorine?
3. What is the test for ammonia?
4. What is the gas produced when carbonates react with acid?
5. During a flame test, what colour is given by a potassium salt?
6. During a flame test, what colour is given by a barium salt?
7. During a flame test, what colour is given by a sodium salt?

New materials

Many scientists are involved in making new materials. These new materials have special *properties* which make them ideal for different *applications*.

Carbon fibres

Carbon, in the form of graphite, is used to make carbon fibres. These fibres have many useful properties:

- They do not stretch.
- They do not compress.
- They are very unreactive.
- They have low **densities**.

Carbon fibres are often mixed with other materials to give greater strength and stiffness to objects such as racing cars and squash racquets.

Thinsulate

Thinsulate is a very popular insulating material. It is used to make objects like gloves and hats. Thinsulate consists of very small micro fibres.

These fibres are very good at trapping air and this helps to keep you warm, because it stops your body heat from escaping. Their small size means that many fibres can be packed into thin layers of Thinsulate. This keeps you warm by reflecting more body heat.

Gore-tex

Gore-tex consists of a thin membrane which is used to coat fabrics. This membrane has lots of tiny holes. Water vapour from sweat is small enough to fit through these holes and pass out of Gore-tex. Liquid water is to big too get through the holes.

Gore-tex is used to make objects like boots and jackets.

Lycra

Lycra is a very stretchy **man-made** fibre. Small amounts of Lycra are mixed with other fibres to make fabrics that are used to manufacture objects like swimsuits and underwear.

Kevlar

Kevlar is an exceptionally strong, lightweight material that is both flexible and comfortable to wear. It has a huge range of uses including:

- bullet-proof vests
- sports equipment
- the moorings for ships and other naval vessels.

Post-it notes

The material that is used to make Post-it notes sticky but not so sticky that they cannot be removed was a fortunate discovery made by scientists who were trying to improve adhesive tape. The scientists realised that they had discovered a very interesting new material, but it was many years before they were able to work out exactly how to use it.

"remember to make for science test"

Teflon

Teflon was another very useful chemical that was discovered accidentally. Scientists trying to develop new gases found that one particular gas, tetrafluoroethene, polymerised spontaneously to make an exciting new material. Polytetrafluoroethene, better known as Teflon, is both very unreactive and extremely slippery. It has been used in a wide range of applications from space suits to non-stick frying pans.

Smart materials

Smart materials have one or more properties which can be dramatically altered by changes in the environment. Thermochromic materials change colour as the temperature changes. Thermochromic materials are used to make objects like mugs which reveal a new pattern when hot liquids are poured into them.

I ♥ SCIENCE

Nano-materials

Scientists are currently researching the properties of new **nano-materials**. These are substances which contain **just a few hundred atoms** and vary in size from 1 nm to 100 nm. These materials have a very high surface area to volume ratio. Scientists hope that this will allow them to use nano-molecules in exciting ways such as:

- in new computers
- as better catalysts
- in sunscreens.

Buckminsterfullerene C$_{60}$

Fullerenes are another form of the element carbon. Fullerenes consist of **cages of carbon atoms** held together by strong covalent bonds. The most symmetrical and therefore most stable example is buckminsterfullerene which consists of 60 carbon atoms joined together in a series of hexagons and pentagons, much like a leather football. In the future, buckminsterfullerene could be used as a catalyst or a lubricant.

KEY TERMS

Make sure you understand these terms before moving on!

- property
- application
- density
- man-made
- smart materials
- nano-materials

QUICK TEST

1. What is the name of the element found in graphite?

2. What special properties do carbon fibres have?

3. Thinsulate traps air. How does this keep you warm?

4. What is Thinsulate used to make?

5. Describe the consistency of Gore-tex.

6. What is Gore-tex used to make?

7. Why is Kevlar used to make bullet-proof vests?

Use the questions to test your progress. Check your answers on page 111.

1   The table is about limestone and some of the substances that can be made from limestone.

Substance	Information about the substance
A	is made when limestone is heated with silica and soda
B	is made when water is added to calcium oxide
C	is a rock that contains large amounts of calcium carbonate
D	is formed when calcium carbonate is heated

   a) What is the name of substance C?

   ....

   b) What is the chemical name of substance D?

   ....

   c) What is the formula of substance B?

   ....

   d) What is the name of substance A?

   ....

2   Crude oil can be separated into fractions.
   a) What is the name of the process used to separate crude oil into fractions?

   ....

   b) Molecules found in the diesel oil fraction contain about twenty carbon atoms while molecules
      in the petrol fraction have about eight carbon atoms. Tick one box to show how petrol and
      diesel molecules compare.
      Compared with diesel molecules, petrol molecules are:

      more flammable   ☐   more viscous   ☐
      have a higher boiling point ☐   have more carbon atoms   ☐

   c) Some long hydrocarbon molecules can be split into smaller, more useful molecules. What is
      the name of the process used to break up long hydrocarbon molecules into shorter more
      useful hydrocarbons?

   ....

3   Iron is produced in a blast furnace. Place these statements in order to show how iron is
   produced.
   a) Carbon dioxide reacts with carbon to form carbon monoxide.   ☐

   b) The iron is dense and sinks to the bottom of the furnace where it can be removed.   ☐

   c) Carbon reacts with oxygen to form carbon dioxide.   ☐

   d) The carbon monoxide reacts with iron oxide to form iron and carbon dioxide.   ☐

4   This table shows the names of four different metals:

Name of metal
aluminium
iron
copper
titanium

   a) Which two of these metals are more reactive than carbon?

   ....

   b) Which of these metals is extracted from its ore bauxite?

   ....

   c) Which metal can be alloyed to form steel?

   ....

   d) Which of these four metals is the best electrical conductor?

   ....

5   This question is about the Earth's atmosphere and how it has changed.
   a) What is the main gas in today's atmosphere?

   ....

   b) What was the main gas in the Earth's early atmosphere?

   ....

   c) The Earth's early atmosphere was similar to the modern-day atmosphere of which two planets
      in the Solar System?

   ....

   d) The levels of carbon dioxide in the atmosphere have increased steadily over the last two
      hundred years. Why is this?

   ....

   e) What is the name of the problem associated with higher levels of carbon dioxide in the
      atmosphere?

   ....

   f) Scientists are also concerned about the damage that acid rain is causing to the environment.
      Which of these pollutants is responsible for the formation of acid rain? Tick one box.

   CFCs   ☐   non-biodegradable plastics   ☐
   sulphur dioxide   ☐   carbon monoxide   ☐
   carbon dioxide   ☐   soot particles   ☐

6   A science teacher is showing her class how sodium metal reacts with water.
   a) Name one safety precaution that the science teacher should take.

   ....

   b) Write a word equation for the reaction between sodium metal and water.

   ....

Current, charge and resistance

An electric *current* is a flow of *charge*. In metals, the charges are normally carried by electrons.

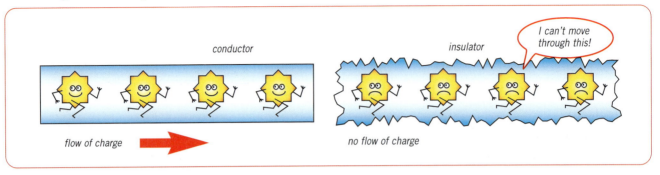

conductor

insulator

I can't move through this!

flow of charge

no flow of charge

Measuring current

We **measure current** with an **ammeter**. The size of a current is the **rate at which the charge is flowing**. The greater the flow rate, the larger the current.

Charge is measured in coulombs (C). **Current (I)** is measured in **amps** or **amperes (A)**. 1 A is a flow rate of 1 C/s. If a current of 3 A

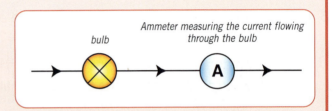

bulb

Ammeter measuring the current flowing through the bulb

A

passes through a bulb, 3 C of charge flows through it every second.

Making charges flow

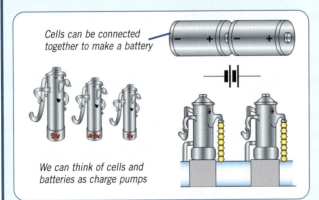

Cells can be connected together to make a battery

We can think of cells and batteries as charge pumps

Cells and **batteries** act as **charge pumps** giving the charges **energy.** Several cells connected together can give more energy to the charges and produce a larger current in the circuit.

Several cells connected together are called a **battery**. The **voltage** of a cell or battery tells us how **much energy** is being given **to each coulomb of charge**. A **1 volt cell** gives **1 joule**

of energy to **each coulomb of charge** that passes through it. A 9 V battery gives 9 J of energy to each coulomb of charge, etc.

Some have labels which indicate their **battery capacity** in amp-hours, e.g. a 40 amp-hour battery will deliver a current of 1 A for 40 hours, or a current of 2 A for 20 hours, etc. before becoming flat.

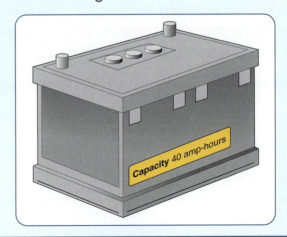

Capacity 40 amp-hours

Using solar cells

Cells and batteries produce **direct current**. Direct current is current which **flows in just one direction**. Solar cells can also be used to produce direct current. Solar cells change light energy into electrical energy.

Devices which require low currents, such as this calculator, may use solar cells as their source of energy. Solar cells are also used to produce electrical energy for devices in remote regions such as on the tops of mountains and in space.

Solar cell

KEY TERMS

Make sure you understand these terms before moving on!

- current
- charge
- coulomb
- amps/amperes
- cell
- battery
- voltage
- battery capacity
- direct current

QUICK TEST

1. What is an electric current?
2. What instrument do we use to measure current?
3. What is a battery?
4. A battery has a capacity of 20 amp-hours. For approximately how long can a current of 4 A be supplied by this battery?
5. What is 'direct current'?
6. What does a solar cell do?
7. Give one example where solar cells may be used.

Electrical resistance

Resistance

Components in a circuit **resist current** flowing through them. They have **resistance**. If current can pass easily through a component, we say it has a low resistance. We measure the resistance of a component in **ohms** (Ω). If a **current** of 1 A flows when a **voltage** of 1 V is applied across a component, the component has a resistance of 1 Ω.

We can write this statement as a formula:

$$V = I \times R$$

Example

Calculate the voltage that must be applied across a wire of resistance 4 Ω if a current of 3 A is to flow.

$$V = I \times R = 3 \text{ A} \times 4 \text{ }\Omega = 12 \text{ V}$$

 $V = I \times R$ is an important equation and is often needed in exams.

Using resistors

Resistors are components that are put into a circuit because of their resistance. We can use **resistors** to **control the size of the current** flowing in a circuit.

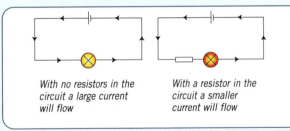

With no resistors in the circuit a large current will flow

With a resistor in the circuit a smaller current will flow

If a **variable resistor** is included in a circuit, its value can be altered so that the current flowing in a circuit can easily be changed. **Dimmer switches** are variable resistors which are used to control the brightness of your lights.

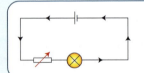

Altering the value of this variable resistor changes the brightness of the bulb

Current/voltage graphs 1

If a range of voltages is applied across a piece of wire (or a resistor) and the currents that flow through it are measured, a **current-voltage graph** can be drawn for the wire. Providing the temperature of the wire does not change, the graph will be a **straight-line graph passing through the origin**.

This shape of graph shows that the **current** flowing through the wire is **directly proportional to the voltage**: if we double the voltage the current is also doubled. Some components in a circuit do not produce straight-line graphs, e.g. filament bulbs.

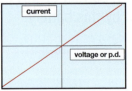

I/V graph for an ohmic conductor, e.g. length of wire. The steeper the line the lower the resistance

current

voltage or p.d.

Altering the variable resistor changes the p.d. across the wire

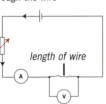

The ammeter measures the current passing through the wire

length of wire

The voltmeter measures the p.d. across the wire

Current/voltage graphs 2

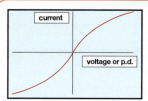

I/V graph for a filament bulb. As the current is increasing the resistance is increasing so the graph becomes flatter

As the current flowing through the filament of the bulb increases, its temperature increases and so does its resistance.

Special resistors you need to know about

Light dependent resistors (LDRs)

- These have a **high resistance** when there is **little or no light** shining on them.
- Their **resistance decreases** as **light intensity increases**.
- They are used in **light-sensitive circuits**, e.g. for controlling **street lighting, in burglar alarms or in digital cameras to control how long a shutter should be open**.

Thermistors

- These are resistors **whose resistance alters greatly as their temperature changes**.
- Unlike wires, the vast majority of these resistors have **resistances that decrease** as their **temperature increases**.
- They are used in **temperature-sensitive circuits**, e.g. **fire alarms and thermostats**.

Examiners like to ask questions about the effects of having certain types of resistor in circuits. Make sure you know about all the different types and what they can do.

Simple burglar alarm

light-dependent resistor (LDR)   buzzer

If the burglar turns on the light the resistance of the LDR falls. Current now flows around the circuit and the buzzer sounds

Simple fire alarm

thermistor

As the thermistor becomes warm its resistance falls. Current now flows around the circuit and the buzzer sounds

KEY TERMS

Make sure you understand these terms before moving on!

- resistance
- variable resistor
- proportional
- light-dependent resistor (LDR)
- thermistor

QUICK TEST

1. In what units do we measure resistance?

2. Give one use for a variable resistor.

3. Calculate the voltage which must be applied across a wire of resistance 100 Ω in order that a current of 0.12 A flows.

4. What type of resistor is affected by the intensity of light? Give one use for this type of resistor.

5. What type of resistor decreases its resistance as its temperature increases? Give one use for this type of resistor.

Generating electricity

Induced voltage/current

- If a wire is moved across a magnetic field (at right angles), a voltage is **induced** in the wire and a **current will flow**.
- If the **wire** is moved in the **opposite direction**, the induced voltage and induced current are in the **opposite direction**.
- To **increase the size** of the voltage/current we could:
  a) use **a stronger magnet** or
  b) move the wire **more quickly**.
- If the wire is held **stationary** or moved **parallel** to the field, **no voltage or current** is induced.
- If a **magnet is moved into a coil**, a **voltage/current is induced** in it.
- If the **magnet is pulled out** the voltage/current is in **the opposite direction**.

- To increase the size of the voltage/current we can:
  a) use a **stronger magnet**
  b) **move the magnet faster**
  c) put **more turns on the coil**.

In both experiments, the induced voltage or current is created **when magnetic lines of force** are being cut by a conductor, such as a piece of wire. If no **magnetic lines are being cut**, there is **no induced voltage/current**. These observations were described by Faraday. He found that the faster the cutting of the field lines by a conductor, the larger the voltage or current induced.

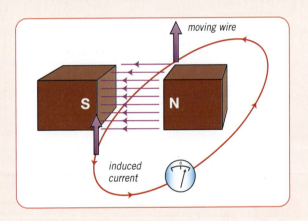

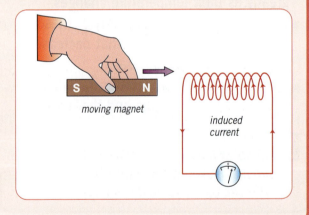

Power stations

Coal, oil and gas are **non-renewable fuels**. When we burn them we produce gases that pollute our atmosphere, causing **acid rain** and **global warming**.

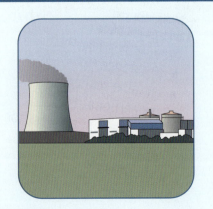

Generators and alternators

- If a **coil is rotated** between the poles of a magnet, a **current is induced** in the coil.
- Because the wires are continually **changing direction** as they rotate, the **induced current** also **changes size and direction**.
- The induced current is **an alternating current**.
- A **generator** which produces **alternating current** is called an **alternator**.
- The coil will generate a larger current if:
  a) a **stronger magnet** is used
  b) the coil is **turned more quickly**
  c) a coil with **more turns** is used.

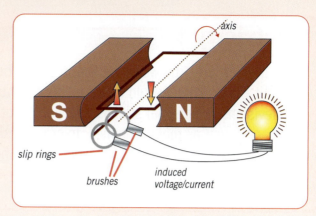

slip rings
brushes
induced voltage/current
axis

> *Don't let phrases like 'induced current' confuse you.*
> *Just try to understand how voltages and currents can be made using magnetic fields and wires.*

The simple dynamo

A **dynamo**, like that used on a bicycle, is **used to generate small currents**.

- As the **wheel rotates**, the magnet and its **magnetic field spin around**.
- Its **magnetic lines of force cut through the coil** inducing a current in it.
- The **current generated keeps changing size and direction**. It is called an **alternating current**.
- This current can be used to work the bicycle's lights.
- If the cyclist stops, the **wheel stops**, there is **no movement of the magnet** and its field, so there is **no induced current** and the **lights will go out**.

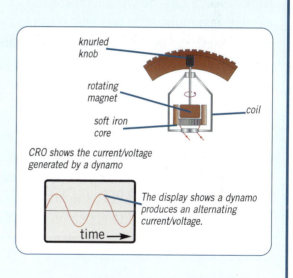

knurled knob
rotating magnet
soft iron core
coil

CRO shows the current/voltage generated by a dynamo

The display shows a dynamo produces an alternating current/voltage.

time →

KEY TERMS

Make sure you understand these terms before moving on!

- induced voltage
- induced current
- magnetic lines of force
- non-renewable fuels
- acid rain
- global warming
- generator
- alternator
- dynamo
- alternating current

QUICK TEST

1. What kind of current is produced when a magnet is rotated inside a coil?

2. Suggest two ways in which an alternator can be changed to produce a higher current.

3. Name one type of environmental damage that might be caused as a result of using fossil fuels in our power stations.

The impact of electricity

Electricity

Without electricity, the world we live in would be a very different place. There would be no electric lights or heating, no televisions or personal stereos. We would not have **electrical appliances** such as mobile phones, microwave ovens and washing machines. Since its discovery several hundred years ago electricity has had a huge impact on our lives, but not always in a positive way!

Impact of electricity on communications

Many of the improvements in our ability to communicate would have been impossible without electricity. Before the nineteenth century, communication was only possible by written word, i.e. by letter, or by travelling and speaking directly to the person you wanted to communicate with.

By the early nineteenth century, messages could be sent more quickly and over long distances using **Morse code** and the **telegraph**. Towards the end of the nineteenth century, the **telephone** had been invented and, by 1880, the first public telephone boxes started to appear in the UK.

In the 1920s, the first radio broadcasts were made. Television broadcasts began in 1936. In the 1970s we had the first cell phones (mobile phones). Now, at the beginning of the twenty-first century, there are over three billion mobile phones in use worldwide. Since the 1970s, the **Internet** has become established as one of the key methods of modern-day communications.

Smaller and faster

The first **computers**, like the one above, were built in the 1950s. They consisted of rows and rows of thermionic valves. The computers took several minutes to warm up, needed a lot of power, took up great deal of room and were very slow, even when carrying out the simplest of calculations.

Towards the end of the 1950s and the beginning of the 1960s, the **space race** was driving many areas of technology to produce electrical circuits that were smaller, faster and more reliable than their predecessors. This resulted in the thermionic valve being replaced by the **transistor** and **integrated circuits (ICs)** replacing individual components and their wiring. ICs have made computers, video recorders, washing machines, etc. so cheap that almost every home in the country has one and has come to rely on them.

Batteries

There are two main types of batteries: **rechargeable** and **non-rechargeable**. Although rechargeable batteries have the advantage that they can be used many times over, they do not last forever and eventually, like non-rechargeable batteries, they have to be disposed of. Last year, over 20 000 tonnes of household batteries were thrown away in the UK.

Some of these batteries contain dangerous metals, such as cadmium (which affects the kidneys and can cause cancer), mercury (which can cause brain damage) and lead (which affects the nervous system and can also cause brain damage). Great care must, therefore, be taken with used batteries.

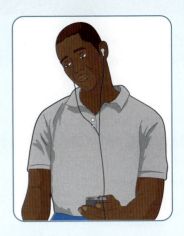

Devices such as this MP3 player, which use batteries as a source of electricity, have given us all a greater degree of freedom. This would not have been possible without the recent developments in battery technology, but there is a cost

KEY TERMS

Make sure you understand these terms before moving on!

- electrical appliances
- Morse code
- telegraph
- transistor
- integrated circuit (IC)
- rechargeable battery
- non-rechargeable battery

QUICK TEST

1. Name three electrical appliances that have changed the life of the average person.

2. What system of communicating over long distances was used in the early nineteenth century?

3. Which two systems of communicating were developed in the latter part of the twentieth century?

4. Why was there a sudden drive in the 1960s to produce smaller and faster circuits?

5. Name one disadvantage of using batteries as a source of electricity.

Renewable sources of energy

Fossil fuels such as coal, oil and gas are rich sources of energy but they are non-renewable. They will not last forever. There are, however, some sources of energy which will not run out. These are called *renewable sources of energy*. Why don't we make more use of these renewable sources? Each of these sources has advantages and disadvantages to their use. These should be considered carefully before any choice is made.

Wind power

The **kinetic energy of the wind** is used to drive turbines and generators.

✓ It is a **renewable** source of energy and therefore will not be exhausted.
✓ It requires **low-level technology** and therefore can be used by developing countries.
✓ **It produces no atmospheric pollution**.

✗ It causes **visual and noise pollution**.
✗ It is **limited to windy sites**.

Wave power

The kinetic energy of the **rocking motion of the waves** is used to generate electricity.

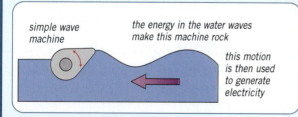

simple wave machine

the energy in the water waves make this machine rock

this motion is then used to generate electricity

✓ It is a **renewable source**.
✓ It produces **no atmospheric pollution**.
✓ It is **useful for isolated islands**.

✗ It has a **high initial cost**.
✗ It causes **visual pollution**.
✗ It has **poor energy capture**. A large area of machines is needed even for a small energy return.

Hydroelectricity

The **kinetic energy of flowing water** is used to drive turbines and generators.

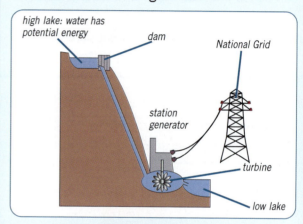

high lake: water has potential energy
dam
National Grid
station generator
turbine
low lake

✓ It is a **renewable source**.
✓ Energy **can be stored** until required.
✓ It produces **no atmospheric pollution**.

✗ It has a **high initial cost**.
✗ It may cause a **high cost to the environment**, i.e. flooding, loss of habitat.

Tidal power

At high tide, water is trapped behind a barrage or dam. When it is released at low tide, the water drives turbines and generates electricity.

✓ It is a **renewable source**.
✓ It is **reliable** – there are always two tides per day.
✓ It causes **no atmospheric pollution**.
✓ It has **low running costs**.

✗ It has a **high initial cost**.
✗ It may cause **damage to the environment**, e.g. flooding.
✗ It can be an **obstacle to water transport**.

Geothermal

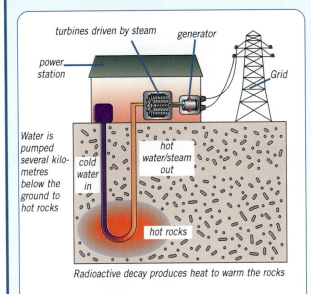

turbines driven by steam

generator

power station

Grid

Water is pumped several kilometres below the ground to hot rocks

cold water in

hot water/steam out

hot rocks

Radioactive decay produces heat to warm the rocks

In regions where the Earth's crust is thin, **hot rocks beneath the ground** can be used to heat water, turning it into steam. This steam is then used to drive turbines and generate electricity.

✓ It is a **renewable source of energy**.
✓ It causes **no pollution and no environmental problems**.

✗ There are **very few suitable sites**.
✗ There is a **high cost to drilling** deep into the ground.

Biomass

'**Things that have grown**', e.g. wood, can be **burned** to release energy. This energy source can be maintained by growing a succession of trees and cropping them when they mature.

✓ It is a **renewable source of energy**.
✓ **Trees are easy to grow and harvest** and are useful, therefore, in developing countries.

✗ **A large area of land is needed** to grow sufficient numbers of trees.

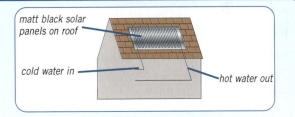

matt black solar panels on roof

cold water in

hot water out

Solar energy

The energy carried in the Sun's rays can be converted directly into electricity using solar cells.

Alternatively, the energy carried in the Sun's rays can be absorbed by dark coloured panels and used to heat water.

✓ It is low maintenance.
✓ It causes no pollution.
✓ There is no need for power cables.

✗ Initially it is quite expensive.
✗ It may not be so useful in regions where there is limited sunshine.

KEY TERMS

Make sure you understand these terms before moving on!

- renewable source of energy
- wind power
- hydroelectricity
- wave power
- tidal power
- geothermal
- biomass
- solar energy

QUICK TEST

1. Why are fossil fuels called non-renewable sources of energy?

2. What is a renewable source of energy?

3. Name three renewable sources of energy.

4. Name three ways in which water could be used as an energy resource.

Electric motors

We use electric motors in almost every area of our lives. Whether we are listening to CDs, watching videos or DVDs, or simply lowering the electric window of a car, we are using an *electric motor*. When we turn a motor on, electrical energy is being used to produce motion. The description below explains how this happens.

Force on a current-carrying wire

If a **current is passed through a wire** which lies **between the poles of a magnet**, there is a force on the wire. If the direction of the current or the direction of the **magnetic field** is changed, the direction of the force on the wire also changes.

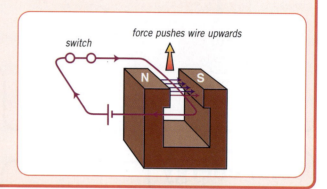

The rotating loop of wire

If the length of wire is replaced by a **loop** of wire when current passes around it, one side of the loop will feel a force trying to push it upwards. There will also be a force on the opposite side of the loop trying to push it downwards. The effect of these two forces is to make the **loop rotate**. This is the basic idea behind the **electric motor**.

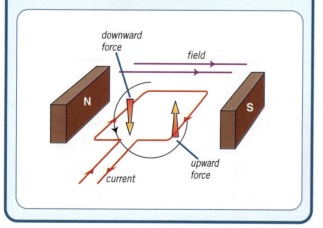

The simple electric motor

For the loop to **rotate continuously,** the direction of the **force** on each side must **change after every half turn**, i.e. first a wire must be pushed up, then it must be pushed down, etc. This change is achieved by using a **split ring commutator**. The split ring **changes the direction of the current** in the coil after **every half turn**.

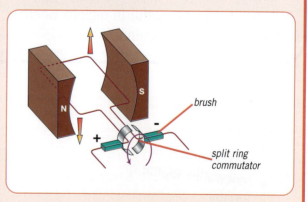

To make a motor turn more quickly we can:

- increase the **current**
- increase the **number of turns on the coil**
- increase the **strength of the magnet**.

Efficiency

Usually, when an energy transfer takes place, only part of the energy is changed into something useful. The remainder is wasted. The table below contains some examples.

Energy input	Device	Useful energy output	Wasted energy
electrical	television	light and sound	heat
chemical	car	kinetic energy	heat and sound
electrical	electric light bulb	light	heat
chemical	candle	light	heat

This wasted energy is transferred to the surroundings, which then become warmer. The greater the percentage of energy that is **usefully transformed** by a device, the more **efficient** the device. We can calculate how efficient a transfer is by using the equation:

$$\text{efficiency} = \frac{\text{useful energy transferred by the device}}{\text{total energy supplied to the device}} \times 100\%$$

Example

An electric motor changes 200 J of electrical energy into 80 J of kinetic energy and 120 J of heat and sound energy. Calculate the efficiency of the motor.

$$\text{efficiency} = \frac{\text{useful energy transferred by the device}}{\text{total energy supplied to the device}} \times 100\%$$

$$= \frac{80\text{ J}}{200\text{ J}} \times 100\%$$

$$= 40\%$$

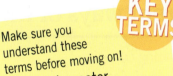

KEY TERMS

Make sure you understand these terms before moving on!

- electric motor
- magnetic field
- split ring commutator
- efficiency

QUICK TEST

1. What energy change takes place in an electric motor?

2. Give two examples of electric motors you might find in your home.

3. What happens to a loop of wire that experiences an upward force on one side and a downward force on the other side?

4. Which device changes the direction of the current in an electric motor every half turn?

5. List three ways of increasing an electric motor's rate of rotation.

6. Calculate the efficiency of an electric motor that changes 300 J of electrical energy into 150 J of kinetic energy.

Insulate your home efficiently

Insulating your home

This diagram shows how heat may escape from your house if it has not been insulated.

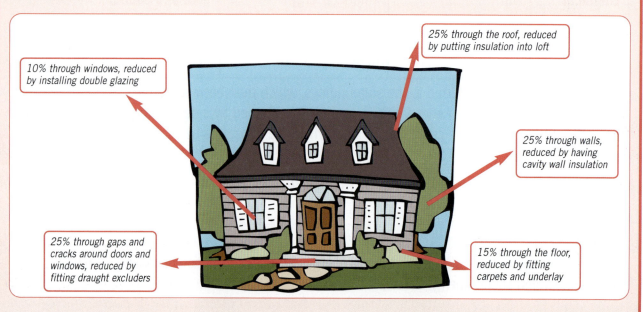

10% through windows, reduced by installing double glazing

25% through the roof, reduced by putting insulation into loft

25% through walls, reduced by having cavity wall insulation

25% through gaps and cracks around doors and windows, reduced by fitting draught excluders

15% through the floor, reduced by fitting carpets and underlay

To prevent/reduce this loss of energy, your house needs insulating. Which methods of home **insulation** are most **cost-effective**? How can you best invest your money in order to reduce energy loss?

Different ways of insulating your home 1

Double glazing consists of two panes of glass with a small gap between them.
The air trapped in the gap reduces heat loss through the windows by conduction.

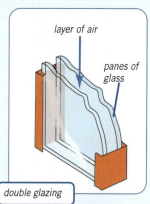

layer of air

panes of glass

double glazing

Cavity wall insulation consists of two walls between which there is foam or fibre containing lots of trapped air.
The trapped air reduces heat loss through the walls by conduction.

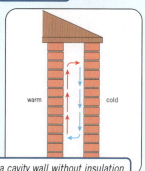

warm   cold

heat loss through a cavity wall without insulation

Loft insulation is often in the form of fibreglass which contains lots of trapped air. This prevents heat loss out of the roof of the house.

loft insulation

Draught excluders are strips of foam or rubber fitted to the sides or bottoms of doors and windows to prevent heat loss. Hanging curtains will also reduce heat loss.

Different ways of insulating your home 2

The table below shows the cost of these different types of insulation and the annual savings that might result from each.

Type of insulation	Typical cost	Typical annual saving	Payback time*
Double glazing	£3000	£150	20 years
Cavity wall	£500	£100	5 years
Loft insulation	£250	£125	2 years
Draught excluders	£60	£20	3 years

* This is the time it takes for a householder to get back the money invested in insulating the house in order to reduce energy losses.

From this table we can draw some important conclusions:

■ The money spent on insulating the loft will be recovered in just two years as a result of the reduction in energy loss.

■ Cavity wall insulation saves a great deal of energy but, because it is expensive, it will take five years before its cost is recovered through reduction of heat loss through walls.

■ Draught excluders are not very expensive and do not save much energy each year, but because they are cheap, they pay for themselves in just three years.

■ Double glazing is a very expensive way of insulating your home. It takes a long time to recover this investment. There may be, however, other reasons for investing in double glazing, e.g. it also provides noise insulation.

> *Make sure you understand the idea of cost-effectiveness. A question about the cost-effectiveness of different types of insulation is asking how quickly the savings will pay for the extra insulation. It is not asking which is the best insulator.*

KEY TERMS

Make sure you understand these terms before moving on!

■ insulation
■ cost-effectiveness
■ double glazing
■ cavity wall
■ loft insulation
■ draught excluder

QUICK TEST

1. What is an insulator?

2. What is double glazing?

3. Suggest five methods by which you could reduce the heat escaping from your house?

4. Using the table on the right, work out the payback time and then a rank order for the cost-effectiveness of the different methods of insulating your home.

Type of insulation	Typical cost	Typical annual saving	Payback time*	Rank order
Double glazing	£4000	£100		
Cavity wall	£800	£80		
Loft insulation	£210	£70		
Draught excluders	£120	£30		

5. Explain why hanging curtains in front of a window reduces heat loss.

Electrical power

All *electrical appliances* transfer electrical energy into other forms. A hairdryer transfers electrical energy into heat and kinetic, and some sound energy. A radio transfers electrical energy into sound energy. The *power* of an appliance is a measure of how quickly these energy changes take place. Power is measured in *watts* (W).

The meaning of power

If a light bulb has a **power rating of 40 W**, it transfers **40 J of electrical energy** into heat and light energy **every second.**

If an electrical fire has a **power rating of 2 kW** (2000 W) it **transfers 2000 J of electrical energy** into 2000 J of heat and light energy **every second.**

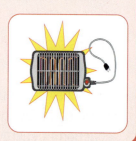

Calculating the power of an appliance

The power rating of an appliance can be calculated using the formula:

Power = Voltage x Current   or   P = V x I

Example
When a voltage of 240 V is applied across a bulb, a current of 0.25 A flows. What is the power rating of this bulb?

P = V x 1 = 240 x 0.25 = 60 W

Kilowatt-hours and units

The electricity supplier measures the energy we use in the home in **kilowatt-hours (kWh)** or **units**. They calculate this value using the formula:

energy used in kilowatt-hours = power in **kilowatts (kW)** x time in hours

Example
Calculate the energy used when a 3 kW fire is turned on for two hours.

E = P x t = 3 kW x 2 hours = 6 kWh or 6 units

The meter and the bill

Somewhere in your house is **a meter** like the one shown on the right. It shows how many units of **electrical energy have been used**. We usually pay our electricity bills every three months, i.e. every quarter. By reading the meter at the beginning and end of the quarter, we can calculate how many units of electrical energy have been used.

Electricity Bill				
Charges for electricity used				
Present reading 80839	**Previous reading** 80039	**Units used** 800	**Pence per unit** 11.00	**Charge amount** £88.00
Quarterly standing charge				£12.00
Total				£100.00

The bill shows the **number of units used** and the **cost per unit**. By multiplying these two values together, we can obtain the cost of the electrical energy used.

The electricity supplier will also add a **standing charge** to your bill. This pays for the equipment used by the supplier in bringing the electricity into your home and its maintenance.

KEY TERMS

Make sure you understand these terms before moving on!

- electrical appliance
- power
- watt (W)
- kilowatt-hour (kWh)
- unit
- kilowatt (kW)

Example

The readings on an electricity meter at the beginning and end of a quarter show that a family has used 800 units. If the cost of one unit is 11 pence and the standing charge per quarter is £12.00, calculate the total bill for this household.

> cost of electricity = number of units used x cost per unit = 800 x 11p = £88.00

If the standing charge is £12.00, the total cost of the bill is £88.00 + £12.00 = £100.00

QUICK TEST

1. How many kilowatt-hours (units) of electrical energy are converted into other forms in the following situations?

   a) 3 kW fire turned on for three hours

   b) 2 kW tumble dryer used for 30 minutes

   c) 1.5 kW water heater turned on for two hours

   d) 500 W TV turned on for four hours

   e) 100 W radio turned on for 10 hours

2. Calculate the power of an electric fire if a current of 12.5 A flows when it is connected to a 240 V supply.

Domestic electricity

The electricity we use in the home is known as *mains electricity*. It is generated at a power station and then transmitted to us through the *National Grid*. It is different from the electricity we use from cells and batteries in several ways.

a.c./d.c.

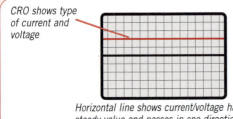

CRO shows type of current and voltage

Horizontal line shows current/voltage has a steady value and passes in one direction. This is a d.c. current from a cell or battery

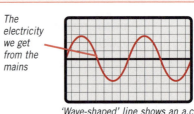

The electricity we get from the mains

'Wave-shaped' line shows an a.c. current/voltage which is continually changing direction

The electricity we get from cells and batteries is **one-way electricity**. It is called **direct current (d.c.)**. The electricity from the mains is **continuously changing direction**. It is **alternating current (a.c.)**. It flows **back and forth 50 times every second**, i.e. it has a **frequency of 50 Hz**.

The three-pin plug

The voltage of the electricity from cells and batteries is quite low, e.g. 9 V, 12 V, etc. **The voltage from the mains is about 230 V. It can be dangerous if not used safely. Most appliances** are therefore **connected** to the mains using **insulated plugs**.

It is very important that the wires in a plug are connected to **the correct pins**. Looking at an open plug like the one shown below, the **BRown** wire goes to the **Bottom Right** and the **BLue** wire goes to the **Bottom Left**. The green and yellow wire (earth) goes to the pin at the top.

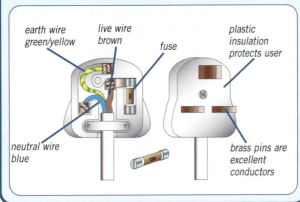

earth wire green/yellow

live wire brown

fuse

plastic insulation protects user

neutral wire blue

brass pins are excellent conductors

Fuses

All three-pin UK plugs contain a **fuse**. This usually consists of a small **cylinder or cartridge** containing a thin piece of **wire with a low melting point**.

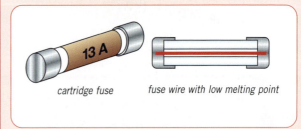

cartridge fuse

fuse wire with low melting point

If a fault develops in a circuit and **too much current passes** through the fuse, the **wire melts**. The circuit becomes **incomplete** and **current ceases to pass through it**. The fuse **protects the user** and **limits any damage** to the electrical appliance.

Fuses are given a **rating**, which indicates the **maximum current** that can flow through it without it melting. The most common fuses in the UK have ratings of **1 A, 3 A and 13 A**.

Which fuse?

Choosing the correct value of **fuse** for a circuit is important. If the fuse selected has too low a rating, it will melt (blow) and turn off the circuit, even when there is no fault and the correct current is flowing. If the fuse has too high a rating it will not protect the circuit when too large a current flows. The correct value of fuse is one that is **just large enough to allow the correct current to flow**, e.g. if the normal current is 2 A then a 3 A fuse is selected.

The earth wire

A three-pin plug usually has three wires connected to it. The **electrical energy** travels into an appliance **through the live wire**. The **neutral wire** is the **return path** for the current. The **earth wire** is a safety connection, which **protects the user** if an appliance becomes faulty.

If a kettle has a metal casing and the heating element is broken, anyone touching the casing will receive **an electrical shock**. With the **earth wire connected**, the user is safe and will not receive an electric shock. Modern kettles now have **plastic casings** to further reduce the risk of an electric shock for the user. This is called **double insulation**.

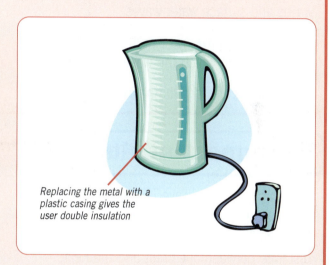

Replacing the metal with a plastic casing gives the user double insulation

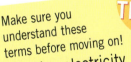

Make sure you understand these terms before moving on!

- mains electricity
- National Grid
- direct current (d.c)
- alternating current (a.c)
- fuse
- live wire
- neutral wire
- earth wire
- double insulation

QUICK TEST

1. What kind of current is supplied through the mains?

2. Why do we put fuses in a circuit?

3. What are the values of the most common fuses used in the UK?

4. Why do we have an earth wire in most mains circuits?

5. What kind of protection is provided by a kettle which has a plastic outer casing?

Waves

Longitudinal and transverse waves

Waves transfer energy by vibrations. There are two main types of waves. They are **transverse waves** and **longitudinal waves**.

A **transverse wave** has vibrations across or at right angles to the direction in which the wave is moving.

Examples of transverse waves include light waves and surface water waves.

A **longitudinal wave** has vibrations that are along the direction in which the wave is moving.

Sound waves are longitudinal waves.

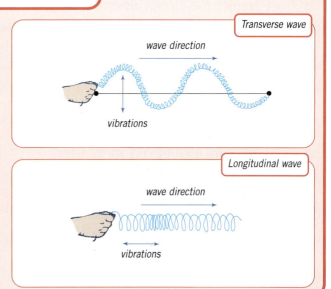

Transverse wave

wave direction

vibrations

Longitudinal wave

wave direction

vibrations

The important bits

The **amplitude** of a wave is the height of a crest or depth of a trough from the undisturbed position. The **wavelength** of a wave is the distance between one crest and the next.

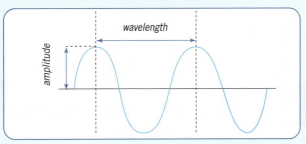

wavelength

amplitude

The **frequency** of a wave is the number of complete waves produced each second by the source. It is measured in hertz **(Hz)**. A wave has a frequency of 200 Hz if the source is producing 200 waves each second.

We can also describe the frequency of a wave as being the number of waves which passes a point each second.

The velocity of a wave (v), its frequency (f) and its wavelength (λ) are related by the equation:

$$v = f \times \lambda$$

Example
A sound wave has a frequency of 170 Hz and a wavelength of 2 m. Calculate the velocity of this wave.

$$v = f \times \lambda = 170 \times 2$$
$$= 340 \text{ m/s}$$

Seismic waves

Seismic waves are **shock waves** caused by **earthquakes**. They travel through the Earth starting from the **epicentre**. Seismic waves can cause tremendous damage to buildings and structures on the Earth's surface. They can also create extremely large and dangerous waves called **tsunami**. If we understand earthquakes and seismic waves better we may be able to give early warnings of these dangers.

There are two types of seismic waves. They are called **P-waves** and **S-waves**.

P-waves

- They are **longitudinal waves** that can travel through **solids and liquids**.
- They cause the surface of the Earth and buildings to vibrate **up and down**.
- They travel slightly **faster than S-waves**.
- **The denser** the material through which they are travelling, the **faster** they travel.

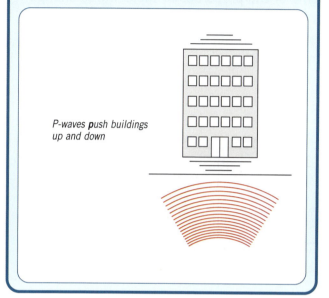

*P-waves **p**ush buildings up and down*

S-waves

- They are **transverse waves** that can **only travel through solids, not through liquids**.
- They cause **side-to-side vibrations** on the surface.
- They travel slightly more **slowly than P-waves**.
- **The denser** the material through which they are travelling, the **faster** they travel.

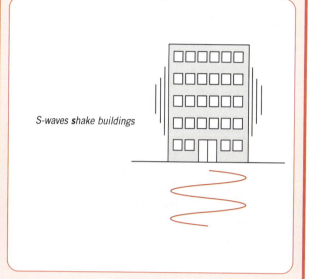

*S-waves **s**hake buildings*

> ⓘ *Make sure you can explain the main features of a wave, i.e. its frequency, wavelength and amplitude.*

KEY TERMS

Make sure you understand these terms before moving on!

- transverse wave
- longitudinal wave
- amplitude
- wavelength
- frequency
- seismic wave
- P-wave
- S-wave

QUICK TEST

1. What do waves carry from place to place?
2. Explain the phrase 'a wave has a frequency of 25 Hz'.
3. Give one example of a) a transverse wave; b) a longitudinal wave.
4. A water wave has a frequency of 5 Hz and a wavelength of 3 m. Calculate the velocity of this wave.
5. What are the names of the two different types of waves produced by an earthquake?
6. Name three differences between these waves.

The electromagnetic spectrum

The electromagnetic spectrum

The **electromagnetic spectrum** is a family of waves with a large number of common properties.

They are all able to travel through a vacuum. They all travel at the same speed through a vacuum, i.e. the speed of light. They are all transverse waves. They all transfer energy.

They can all be reflected, absorbed, transmitted, refracted and diffracted.

Some of the properties of these waves change as the wavelength and frequency change. The family is, therefore, divided into seven smaller groups.

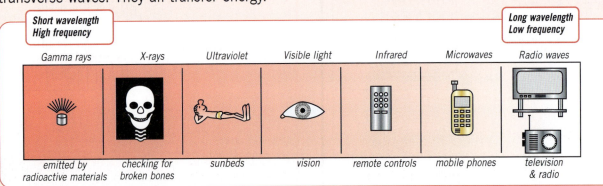

Short wavelength High frequency | Long wavelength Low frequency

| Gamma rays | X-rays | Ultraviolet | Visible light | Infrared | Microwaves | Radio waves |

| emitted by radioactive materials | checking for broken bones | sunbeds | vision | remote controls | mobile phones | television & radio |

Radio waves

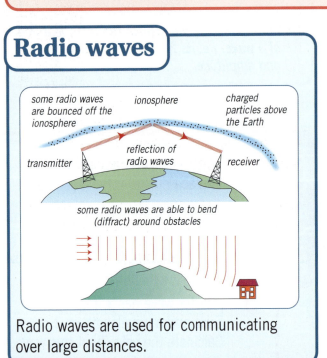

some radio waves are bounced off the ionosphere

ionosphere

charged particles above the Earth

reflection of radio waves

transmitter   receiver

some radio waves are able to bend (diffract) around obstacles

Radio waves are used for communicating over large distances.

Microwaves

Some microwaves pass easily through the Earth's atmosphere and so are used for **communications via satellites, e.g. mobile phones**. Some microwaves are used for **cooking, e.g. microwave ovens**. Water molecules inside food absorb microwaves and become 'hot', cooking the food from the inside.

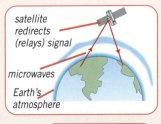

satellite redirects (relays) signal

microwaves

Earth's atmosphere

water in food absorbs microwaves

Infrared waves (also known as heat radiation) 1

Infrared waves are **given out by all warm objects**. The photograph on the right is called a **thermogram**. It was taken using the infrared radiation emitted by the building.

The **different colours indicate different temperatures**. The lighter colours are the hottest parts of the building and the coldest parts are blue. Photographs like this are very useful to identify where heat is being lost from a building.

Infrared waves (also known as heat radiation) 2

Remote controls for TVs, radios, etc. use infrared waves to carry instructions.

Infrared waves carry the instruction from the remote to the TV

Ultraviolet

Ultraviolet waves are **emitted by the Sun.** They cause our skin to tan. We divide ultraviolet light into three smaller groups: UVA, UVB and UVC. When certain chemicals are exposed to ultraviolet, they **fluoresce** (**glow**). Words written with security markers are only visible in ultraviolet light. Ultraviolet light can be used to scan for forged banknotes. When the ultraviolet light is absorbed by the ink, light is emitted and the ink seems to glow. This fluorescence will show if the banknote is a forgery.

Gamma rays

These **very penetrating waves** are **emitted by some radioactive materials**. They can be used to kill harmful bacteria, e.g. sterilise surgical equipment. If used correctly, they can also be used to kill certain kinds of cancer, e.g. with radiotherapy.

Visible light

We use these waves **to see**. It is the one part of the electromagnetic spectrum to which our **eyes are sensitive**. Visible light is used to carry messages down **optical fibres**.

Visible light is used in **iris recognition** security systems.

The patterns in your iris are unique. These are scanned with visible light and recorded. When security checks are made, your iris is scanned again. The reflected light creates an image which is then compared with the original.

X-rays

X-rays are **highly penetrating**. They can penetrate skin and soft tissue but are absorbed by bone. This is why they are used to look for damaged bones inside the body.

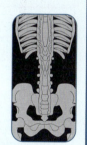

Overexposure can cause cancer. Radiographers, therefore, **stand behind lead screens** or **wear lead aprons to prevent overexposure**. **X-rays** used to be used to monitor the development of a foetus in the womb during pregnancy, but now ultrasound is used, as it is less likely to cause any damage to the unborn baby.

KEY TERMS

Make sure you understand these terms before moving on!

- electromagnetic spectrum
- thermogram
- iris recognition
- fluoresce
- penetrating

QUICK TEST

1. Name two properties all these waves have in common.
2. Name two features of these waves that change as we move from group to group.
3. Name three groups of waves that can be used for communications.
4. Name two groups of waves that can be used for cooking.

More about waves

Our society depends upon waves in many areas of our lives, for communication, in leisure, for medical treatment, etc. It is, therefore, essential that we also recognise the drawbacks and dangers some of these waves may pose if we misuse them.

Biological effects of exposure to electromagnetic waves

Type of wave	Frequency	Effect
Radio waves		No known effect.
Microwaves		Are **absorbed by water molecules** causing body tissue to warm. Large doses **can cause burns**. The rapid increase in the **usage of mobile phones** and the erection of microwave **transmitter masts** close to communities is causing concern over the **possible long-term effects of exposure to microwaves**.
Infrared		Overexposure can cause burning of the skin.
Visible light	INCREASING FREQUENCY	Causes the **chemical changes on the retina** of the eye which makes vision possible. **Overexposure**, e.g. looking directly at the Sun, can cause damage to the retina resulting in impaired vision or blindness.
Ultraviolet		Causes chemical changes in the skin resulting in **tanning and premature ageing**. Excessive exposure will result in **sunburn and possibly skin cancer**. **Sunblocks** help to prevent the radiation from reaching the skin.
X-rays		Highly penetrating rays which can cause **cancer** and kill living cells.
Gamma rays		Emitted by some radioactive materials, they are also very penetrating and can cause damage to or destruction of living cells.

Echoes 1

When sound waves strike a hard surface they are **reflected**. This reflected sound is called an **echo**.

Ships use echoes to find the depth of the ocean beneath them. An **echo-sounder** emits sound waves down towards the sea bed. When the waves strike the sea bed, they are reflected back up to the surface.

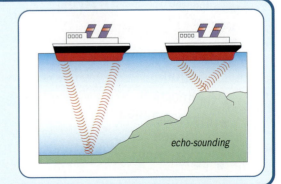

echo-sounding

Echoes 2

A sound detector 'listens' for the echo. The deeper the ocean, the longer it is before the echo is heard. Sound waves used in this way are called **sonar**. This stands for Sound Navigation And Ranging.

Example

A ship emits a sound wave which travels at 1500 m/s through the sea water to the bottom of the ocean. An echo is heard after two seconds. How deep is the ocean?

> Speed = distance / time   or   distance = speed × time
>
> Total distance travelled by the sound wave = 1500 × 2 = 3000 m
>
> The depth of the ocean is, therefore, 1500 m (1500 down and 1500 back up)

Modern sonar equipment uses ultrasounds. Ultrasonic waves can be emitted as a very narrow beam that does not spread out very much as it travels away from the source. Normal sound waves undergo **diffraction** and spread out a lot as they travel through the water. The echoes these waves produce are weaker than those from the ultrasounds and, therefore, are more difficult to detect.

Ultrasonic scanning is carried out in hospitals to monitor the progress of unborn babies in the mother's womb. The **waves are emitted** by a **probe** which is placed against the mother's abdomen. Some of the waves are reflected by the **foetus**. The **reflected waves** are **processed** by a computer which then produces **an image of the foetus** on a monitor. Ultrasounds do this task far **better than X-rays** as they are **completely harmless** to the unborn baby. They can be used to detect abnormalities in the foetus.

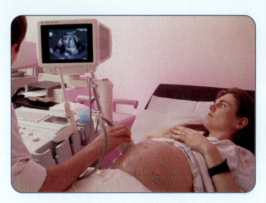

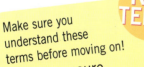
KEY TERMS

Make sure you understand these terms before moving on!

- overexposure
- sunblock
- cancer
- echo
- ultrasonic scanning

QUICK TEST

1. Why are people concerned about the rapid increase in the use of mobile phones?

2. Give one biological effect of overexposure to infrared radiation.

3. Which type of radiation may cause premature ageing of the skin?

4. Suggest one way in which you could limit your exposure to UV light.

5. A ship emits a sound wave which travels at 1500 m/s through the sea water to the bottom of the ocean. An echo is heard after four seconds. How deep is the ocean?

Analogue and digital signals

Total internal reflection and optical fibres

When a ray of light enters a glass block at an angle, it **slows down** and bends towards **the normal**. This change in direction is called **refraction**. When the ray emerges from the block it **speeds up** and bends **away from the normal**.

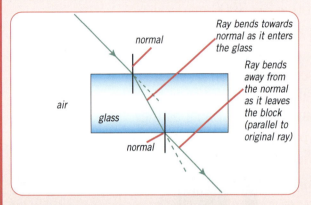

normal

Ray bends towards normal as it enters the glass

Ray bends away from the normal as it leaves the block (parallel to original ray)

air

glass

normal

If a ray leaving a glass block strikes the boundary at an angle **greater than the critical angle**, **total internal reflection** takes place, i.e. the ray is not refracted but reflected.

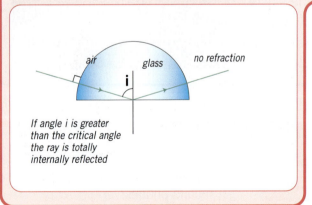

air   glass   no refraction

i

If angle i is greater than the critical angle the ray is totally internally reflected

In modern telecommunications systems, **optical fibres** are being used to replace traditional **copper wires** to carry signals. The light signals in optical fibres undergo total internal reflection.

An optical fibre has a **high-density glass for its core** and a **less dense glass as an outer coating**. The fibre is so narrow that light entering at one end will always strike the boundary between the two glasses at an angle greater than the critical angle. It will, therefore, undergo a **series of total internal reflections** before emerging at the far end.

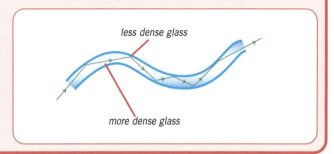

less dense glass

more dense glass

Advantages of using optical fibres

- The fibres are cheaper than copper wires.
- They are lighter.
- They can carry more signals.
- The signals they carry are more secure.

Communicating using analogue signals

As radio waves and microwaves travel from an emitter towards a receiver, there may be some **loss in signal strength**. To ensure that a strong signal arrives at the receiver, it may be **amplified** several times at **repeater stations**.

Analogue signals vary continuously. When they are amplified at repeater stations, any **distortions** (**noise**) which have been added to the wave during its journey will also be **amplified**.

If the noise is considerable, the final signal received may be very different from the original and therefore difficult to understand.

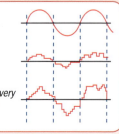

1 Original transmitted signal

2 Weakened signal with noise before amplification

3 Amplified signal and noise – very different from original signal

Communicating using digital signals

An analogue signal can be converted into a **digital signal** so that its shape can be described by a **code consisting of just 1s and 0s**. This code can then be transmitted.

When the weakened signal arrives at a **repeater station**, it is easy to recognise (even with lots of noise) those parts of the signal which should be a 1 and those that should be a 0. These are then amplified, producing a **perfect copy of the original**.

At the receiver, the digital code is converted back into the analogue signal, but without any noise distortion, i.e. the signal is very clear.

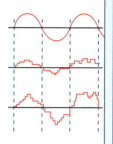

1 Original signal, which has been changed into a digital code before being transmitted

2 Weakened signal, with noise, before amplification

3 Amplified signal, which has had the original code restored – an exact copy of the original transmitted signal

ANALOGUE AND DIGITAL SIGNALS

Physics

KEY TERMS

Make sure you understand these terms before moving on!

- refraction
- critical angle
- total internal reflection
- optical fibre
- repeater station
- analogue signal
- noise
- digital signal

Digital music

Digital signals have had a big influence on the music we listen to and the way in which it is stored.

Electronic keyboards can electronically create the sound waves normally produced by other musical instruments. Sounds produced by instruments can be converted into digital signals and then processed to produce new sounds. CDs and DVDs store music in digital form. MP3 players and iPods receive and store their music and other data in digital form.

> The key things to remember here are the advantages in using digital signals rather than analogue.

QUICK TEST

1. Why is light unable to escape through the sides of an optical fibre?
2. Why do signals need to pass through a repeater station?
3. What is 'noise'?
4. How does noise affect an analogue signal?
5. What is the main advantage of using digital signals rather than analogue?
6. How have digital signals affected the music industry?

The Earth in space

We live on a planet called Earth. It is one of many bodies that together form our *Solar System*.

The Solar System

Our Solar System consists of **a star** and **a number of** planets, **moons**, asteroids and comets. We call our **star the Sun**. It contains over 99% of all the mass in our solar system. The planets, their moons, the asteroids and the comets all orbit the Sun.

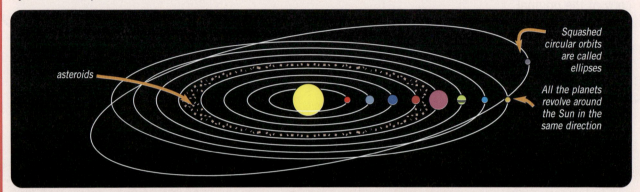

asteroids

Squashed circular orbits are called ellipses

All the planets revolve around the Sun in the same direction

The Earth is one of nine planets. In order, from the planet nearest the Sun, they are: Mercury, Venus, Earth, Mars, Jupiter, Saturn, Uranus, Neptune and Pluto. We can remember the order using the sentence:

Many **V**ery **E**nergetic **M**en **J**og **S**lowly **U**pto **N**ewport **P**agnell.

We see stars like the Sun because of the light they emit. **Stars are luminous** objects. We see **planets and moons** because of the light they reflect. They are **non-luminous objects**.

Gravitational forces

the gravitational pull of the Sun keeps the planets in their orbits

The planets move in orbits because they **are being 'pulled' by the gravity of the Sun**. This force is called a centripetal force. Objects that are closest to the Sun **feel the strongest pull** and follow the **most curved paths**. Objects that are a **long way from the Sun feel the weakest pull** and follow the **least curved orbits**.

Comets

elongated comet orbit

Comets are **large, rock-like pieces of ice** that orbit the Sun. They are thought to have come originally from objects that are orbiting the Sun far beyond the planets. Comets have very elliptical orbits and **travel fastest** when they are **close to the Sun** because the gravitational forces **here are strong**. Close to the Sun, some of a **comet's ice melts, creating a long tail**. Their velocities are lowest when they are a long way from the Sun.

Asteroids

Asteroids are lumps of rock orbiting the Sun. They vary in size from several metres to about 1000 km in diameter. **Most asteroids** are found **in a belt** between **Mars and Jupiter**. Some asteroids are found travelling outside the asteroid belt. If a large asteroid collided with the Earth it could wipe out life as we know it. Is this likely to happen? The answer is yes. It has happened in the past, creating large craters in the Earth's surface. There is no reason to believe that it will not happen in the future, but no one knows when. Hopefully, before it happens, we will have developed the technology to prevent the collision or evacuate the Earth. Some scientists are already suggesting that we set up a programme to look out into space and search for Near Earth Objects (NEOs) that might threaten the Earth.

Interesting, but not to be memorised!

Quite often in an examination you will be given a table of facts and then asked questions about it.

Planet	Distance from Sun in millions of kilometres	Orbit time in Earth years	Mass compared with Earth	Surface temperature in °C	Gravitational field strength in N/kg
Mercury	60	0.2	0.05	350	3.8
Venus	110	0.6	0.80		9.0
Earth	150	1.0	1.00	22	10.0
Mars	230	1.9	0.10	−30	3.8
Jupiter	775	11.9	318	−150	26.4
Saturn	1450	29	95		12.0
Uranus	2900	84	15	−210	9.3
Neptune	4500	165	17		12.0
Pluto	5900	248	0.10	−230	0.3

Try these:

- Name one planet that is closer to the Sun than the Earth.
- Name two planets further away from the Sun than Jupiter.
- Which is the largest planet in our solar system?
- Which planet experiences the strongest gravitational forces?
- Estimate the surface temperatures of Saturn and Neptune.

KEY TERMS

Make sure you understand these terms before moving on!

- Solar System
- star
- planet
- asteroid
- comet
- gravitational forces

QUICK TEST

1. What type of forces keep all the planets in orbit around the Sun?
2. What shape is the orbit of a comet?
3. Where, during their orbit of the Sun, do comets travel fastest?
4. What is an asteroid?
5. What is an NEO and why is it a threat to the Earth?

Stars and the universe

Our Sun is a *star*. It is just one of millions of stars that make up the *galaxy* we live in. Our galaxy is called the *Milky Way*. In the universe there are billions of galaxies. They are separated by distances that are often millions of times greater than the distances between stars within a galaxy.

side view

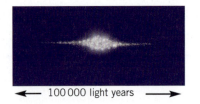

← 100 000 light years →

top view of our galaxy

The Milky Way is a spiral galaxy

← 100 000 light years →

How stars are born

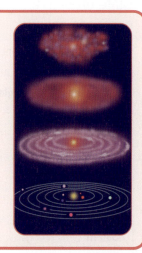

- Stars form when **gravitational forces pull particles of dust and gas together**.
- These forces compress the particles together so tightly that there is a **very large increase in temperature**.
- This temperature increase sets off **nuclear reactions**. These reactions release large amounts of energy as heat and light. As a result, a star is born.
- Smaller **concentrations of gases** may form some distance away from the developing star. These may eventually **become planets and their moons**.

The life of a star 1

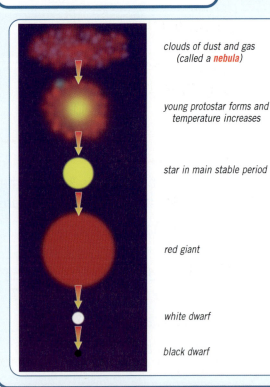

clouds of dust and gas (called a nebula)

young protostar forms and temperature increases

star in main stable period

red giant

white dwarf

black dwarf

Stars change gradually with time.

- When a star first forms, **gravitational forces pull matter together**.
- When the nuclear reactions **begin**, the high temperatures create forces that try to make the **gases expand**.
- When these **two forces are balanced** the star is said to be in its **main stable period**. This period may last for billions of years. Our Sun is in this stable period.
- Towards the end of the stable period, a different type of nuclear reaction begins. As a result, the **star begins to expand** and becomes a little **cooler**. The star is changing into a **red giant**.

The life of a star 2

- Some time later, another, different kind of nuclear reaction begins. On this occasion, the star shrinks to form a **white dwarf**.
- Finally, as a white dwarf **cools** it **changes** into a **cold black dwarf star**.

If a star is much larger than our Sun when in its stable period, it may have a slightly different future. It changes first into a large or super red giant which becomes unstable as it shrinks and cools. An explosion then follows, throwing dust and gas into space. This type of **exploding star** is called a **supernova**.

Any matter which is left behind after the explosion may form a **very dense neutron star or black hole**. The gravity of a black hole is so strong that even **light is unable to escape**.

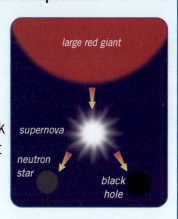

large red giant

supernova

neutron star

black hole

The origins of the universe

Scientists believe that our universe began many billions of years ago with an enormous explosion. This is called the **Big Bang theory**. Even today there is evidence that our universe is still **expanding**. Scientists are now asking whether this expansion will continue forever or whether gravity will gradually slow it down and, perhaps, reverse the process, pulling all matter back to one place (the **Big Crunch**). Perhaps there will be another explosion and the whole process will begin again (the **oscillating model of the universe**). The fate of the universe depends upon how much matter it contains.

> ! *In most of the questions about the planets, stars and the universe, the examiners are keen to see that students understand the importance of gravity. Make sure that you understand the various stages in the birth and life of a star, and how gravity is one of the main forces bringing about these changes.*

KEY TERMS

Make sure you understand these terms before moving on!

- star
- galaxy
- Milky Way
- nebula
- nuclear reactions
- Big Bang

QUICK TEST

1. What is the name of the galaxy in which we live?

2. What forces bring together the particles of dust and gas to form a star?

3. What kinds of reactions cause the temperature of a forming star to increase?

4. What is the final stage in the life of:
   a) a small star;
   b) a very large star?

5. Describe two possible futures for our universe.

Exploring space

Apart from the Earth and the Moon, humans have not visited any of the other bodies in the universe. Nevertheless, we have lots of information about them. Much of this has come from observations made by telescope and data collected by *probes*.

Telescopes

Before the invention of telescopes, all human observations were made with the **unaided eye**. Our view of the universe was very limited. **Optical telescopes** greatly increased our abilities to see new astronomical bodies in our Solar System.

Large optical telescopes similar to the one shown here are often built on mountain tops. Here, the images we see suffer fewer **distortions** from the **Earth's atmosphere** than those at sea level.

Another way to avoid these distortions is to mount **telescopes on satellites** which orbit the Earth high above its atmosphere. A good example of this is the **Hubble telescope** which was launched in 1990. It has seen **further into space** than any previous telescope.

Probes

Flybys are unmanned **probes** which fly **close to** a planet or a moon in order **to gather information**.

Example of a flyby probe – Deep Space 1 was launched in 1998 to fly close to a large asteroid called Braille and study its surface

Landers are unmanned probes which actually **land on the surface of a moon or planet**. They often carry out simple experiments, e.g.

testing soil samples, analysing the planet's or moon's atmosphere, gravitational or magnetic field, etc. They can provide more detailed information than the flyby probes but in general they are **far more expensive**.

Photo taken by Viking 2 Lander showing the surface of Mars

Manned missions

We could gather far more detailed information about neighbouring planets or moons by sending manned probes, but the **extra cost is enormous**. Most of this increase is due to the consideration that has to be given to **providing astronauts with an environment** which will keep them safe for the duration of the trip, for instance:

- There is **no air/oxygen in space**, so this must be taken with them.
- Sufficient **water and food** must also be taken along.
- There must be sufficient **fuel on board for both the outward and return journies**. There is no need for the return journey with an unmanned probe.
- The Earth's atmosphere protects us from cosmic radiation, micrometeorites and much of the Sun's ultraviolet radiation. In space, this is not the case and so **radiation shields** must be included in the spacecraft's design.
- During a journey in space, the gravity will be much less than that experienced on Earth.

In fact, astronauts are likely to experience **weightlessness** most of the time. This can have serious long-term effects on their health. Because astronauts have to do far less work against gravity, this is likely to lead to **calcium depletion**, which may cause bones to become brittle, and **muscle wastage**. The effects of both of these problems may be overcome by astronauts **exercising daily** during the journey or by providing them with 'artificial gravity'.

- Temperatures in space can vary enormously, from −270 °C to in excess of 200 °C. A very narrow temperature range (approximately 10 °C to 30 °C) must be maintained for manned flights. Maintaining this range will also require energy, i.e. for cooling or heating.

Spacecraft

Rocket engines fire **hot gases out** of the back in order to **accelerate forwards**. The size of the reaction force (F) and the acceleration of the rocket (a) are linked by the equation:

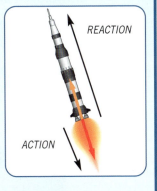

REACTION

ACTION

$F = m \times a$ where m = mass of rocket in kg

Example

Calculate the force that must be applied to a rocket of mass 1000 kg in order to give it an acceleration of 20 m/s^2.

$$F = m \times a$$
$$= 1000 \times 20$$
$$= 20\,000 \text{ N or } 20 \text{ kN}$$

KEY TERMS

Make sure you understand these terms before moving on!

- probe
- optical telescope
- distortions
- flyby
- lander
- weightlessness

QUICK TEST

1. Why are some telescopes built on top of mountains?

2. Explain the difference between a flyby probe and a lander. Give one example of each.

3. Give four reasons why manned flights are much more expensive than unmanned flights.

Why explore space?

Could there be life out there? There are two good reasons to investigate the possibility of life elsewhere in our own Solar System and in other more distant star systems. First if a catastrophic event made the Earth uninhabitable, e.g. the Earth was struck by a large asteroid or comet, we may then be able to find other worlds we could live on. Second, we may be able to make contact with other intelligent life forms that may exist in the galaxy.

Life within our solar system

Planet	Surface temperature in °C	Gravitational field strength (N/kg)	Nature of surface
Mercury	350	4	rocky, almost no **atmosphere**
Venus	480	9	rocky, atmosphere contains CO_2 and sulphuric acid
Earth	22	10	rocky, atmosphere of nitrogen, oxygen and CO_2
Mars	–30	4	rocky, atmosphere of CO_2
Jupiter	–150	27	gas planet, no surface, atmosphere of hydrogen and helium
Saturn	–185	11	gas planet, no surface, atmosphere of hydrogen and helium
Uranus	–210	11	gas planet, no surface, atmosphere of hydrogen and helium
Neptune	–225	12	gas planet, no surface, atmosphere of hydrogen and helium
Pluto	–230	4	almost no atmosphere

From the information above we can see that Mars appears to be the planet in our Solar System with **conditions not dissimilar to those on Earth**. It could, therefore, **support life**.

Unmanned flights to some of the outer planets have discovered other possibilities. For example, Titan and Europa, two of the moons of Saturn, may be habitable.

Titan

Europa

Gravitational field strength

The **mass** of an object is a measure of **how much stuff** (atoms) it contains and is measured in kg. All objects that have mass experience a force when they are placed on a planet or moon. This force is created by the planet's **gravitational field strength**. On Earth, the gravitational field strength is 10 N/kg. This means that an object which has a mass of 1 kg weighs 10 N. A mass of 2 kg will weigh 20 N, etc. We can express this relationship using the equation:

$W = m \times g$ where g = gravitational field strength (or acceleration due to gravity)

Different planets have **different gravitational field strengths** and so objects will have **different weights**.

On Earth my mass is 60 kg and my weight is 600 N
On Mars my mass is still 60 kg but my weight is only 240 N

Planet	Mass of object	Gravitational field strength	Weight of object
Earth	50 kg	10 N/kg	500 N
Mars	50 kg	4 N/kg	200 N
Jupiter	50 kg	27 N/kg	1350 N

On Mars, objects will have less than half their weight on Earth. On Jupiter, they will weigh almost three times as much. Note that the mass of an object does not change when it is moved from planet to planet.

The benefits of space exploration

Exploring space is very costly, but there have been many spin-offs and benefits. These include smoke detectors, weather and communications satellites, space blankets, flat panel TVs, high-power batteries for cordless tools, PTFE, mobile phones, ultrasound scanners, in-car navigation systems and air traffic control collision avoidance systems.

KEY TERMS

Make sure you understand these terms before moving on!

- atmosphere
- mass
- gravitational field strength
- weight

QUICK TEST

1. On which three planets would you weigh the same?

2. On which planet would you weigh the most?

3. Explain why Mars is the most suitable planet for life after the Earth.

4. An object has a mass of 20 kg. What will its weight be on Saturn?

5. Name three benefits of exploring space.

Practice questions

Use the questions to test your progress. Check your answers on page 112.

1   A battery has a capacity of 40 amp-hours. For approximately how long can a current of 4 A be taken from the battery?

   ....

2   What kind of current is produced by a solar cell?

   ....

3   Calculate the voltage across the ends of a 20 Ω resistor when a current of 0.5 A is flowing through it.

   ....

4   What is a light-dependent resistor? Name one use for a light-dependent resistor.

   ....

5   What impact did the space race have on technology in the late 1950s and early 1960s?

   ....

6   Explain the advantages and disadvantages of using batteries as a source of electrical energy.

   ....

7   Name one advantage and one disadvantage of using wind power as your only source of energy for generating electricity.

   ....

8   State three ways in which the speed of rotation of a motor could be increased.

   ....

9   An electric motor changes 500 J of electrical energy into 250 J of kinetic energy. Calculate the efficiency of the motor. Suggest where the other 250 J of energy goes.

   ....

10 The table below lists some ways in which the heating bills for a house could be reduced.

Method	Initial cost	Yearly saving	Payback time
Hot water jacket	£20	£10	
Loft insulation	£300	£60	
Double glazing	£4000	£40	

   a) Calculate the payback time for each of these methods.

   ....

   b) Which method is most cost-effective?

   ....

11 Calculate the electrical energy used in units when a 2 kW fire is turned on for three hours. Calculate the cost of this energy if the cost of one unit is 11p.

   ....

12 Calculate the power of a hairdryer which when connected to a 240 V supply has a current of 5 A flowing through it.

....

13 To which part of an electrical appliance should the earth wire be connected?

....

14 Name three renewable sources of energy.

....

15 A vibrating object produces waves which have a wavelength of 2 m and a frequency of 50 Hz. Calculate the speed of these waves.

....

16 The sequence below shows the electromagnetic spectrum.

A	X-rays	Ultraviolet	Visible light	Infrared	Microwaves	B

a) Name the groups of waves A and B.

....

b) Name three properties which are common to all members of the electromagnetic spectrum.

....

c) Name two groups that could be used for cooking.

....

d) Name two groups that could cause cancer.

....

e) Name one group used for seeing bones inside the body.

....

17 What are seismic waves?

....

18 Name five different types of bodies that make up our Solar System.

....

19 What forces hold the planets in orbits?

....

20 What is the Milky Way?

....

21 What is a supernova?

....

22 Name four ways in which we collect information about our universe.

....

23 Describe three problems astronauts would have to deal with on long, interplanetary flights.

....

Answers

Pages 4–5
1. Energy is lost along the way
2. The numbers of organisms involved in a food chain
3. The mass of the organisms
4. Pyramids of biomass
5. The Sun
6. 10%
7. They need to keep warm
8. Lost in urine and faeces
9. Respiration, heat, waste and parts of the body not eaten
10. Eat lower down in the food chain and intensively rear animals

Pages 6–7
1. Where an organism lives
2. The living things in a habitat
3. Animals and plants
4. Light, space, water and nutrients
5. White (camouflage), thick (insulation) and greasy (doesn't hold water)
6. Only the best adapted organism will survive

Pages 8–9
1. Improved health care, medicine and agriculture
2. Problems in food chains
3. Biological control
4. Building, farming, dumping rubbish and quarrying
5. Cutting down of trees and forests
6. Less carbon dioxide is being absorbed so it builds up in the atmosphere
7. Soil erosion, less rainfall and the destruction of habitats
8. Manure
9. Organic farming, greenhouses and alternative energy sources
10. Organic farming produces less food per area of land so there is less produce grown and it is more time-consuming to develop crops

Pages 10–11
1. Three billion years ago
2. Charles Darwin
3. Environmental change, competition, disease and predators
4. The best adapted
5. Natural selection/survival of the fittest
6. Galapagos Islands off the coast of South America
7. A group of individuals that can breed together to produce fertile offspring
8. He saw that they all showed variation
9. There were more offspring produced than could survive
10. Evolution is a gradual process

Pages 12–13
1. The land changed from marshy to hard ground
2. The dark form as it is camouflaged against predators
3. Oxygen, moisture and warmth
4. They are unable to adapt
5. The remains of dead organisms that have not decayed which lived millions of years ago
6. Yes, because there is an absence of warmth
7. Mutation caused by pollution from factories
8. By destroying habitats, hunting or pollution
9. Near to the surface with older fossils further down in the rock
10. Natural selection

Pages 14–15
1. Breeding animals or plants together to produce the best offspring
2. Artificial selection involves humans doing the selecting rather than nature
3. Genetically identical individuals
4. In the hope that the offspring (foals) will inherit the father's speed and agility
5. Taking cuttings and tissue culture
6. A reduction in the number of alleles
7. Asexual reproduction
8. There are dangers of infertility and health problems if they are closely related
9. Asexual reproduction

Pages 16–17
1. Chromosomes
2. Proteins and enzymes
3. Sections of DNA that code for a particular characteristic
4. On the chromosomes
5. If they occur in reproductive cells
6. 46, nucleus
7. Two
8. Sperms and eggs
9. Sexual reproduction and the environment

Pages 18–19
1. Letters
2. Because they inherit different genes
3. The weaker allele
4. The stronger allele
5. Amount of sunlight and moisture, temperature and mineral content of the soil
6. Random inheritance of parental genes and environmental effects
7. No, their characteristics are affected by the environment
8. Use a Punnett square
9. Alternative forms of a gene
10. Blood group

Pages 20–21
1. Where the genes from one organism are removed and inserted into the cells of another organism
2. They could be grown in cold countries throughout the year
3. A map of all human genes
4. They could mutate into harmful bacteria
5. The use of genetic engineering to treat inherited diseases

Pages 22–23
1. Central nervous system
2. A gap between neurones that transmits the nerve impulse
3. Sensory neurone
4. Motor neurone
5. Relay neurone

Pages 24–25
1. Brain or spinal cord
2. Three
3. A stimulus or change in the environment
4. Yes
5. To protect us from harm
6. Reflex actions are automatic, voluntary actions you have to think about
7. Yes, for example if you are holding a really expensive hot plate and can't drop it until you reach the table where you can put it down
8. The receptor detects the stimulus
9. Motor neurone
10. Sensory

Pages 26–27
1. In the bloodstream
2. Ovaries
3. Luteinising hormone (LH) and follicle stimulating hormone (FSH)
4. Maintaining the body at normal levels, making constant adjustments
5. Convert it to glycogen for storage
6. Glucagon
7. Insulin
8. Attention to diet and injections of insulin

Pages 28–29
1. They slow down the brain and make you feel sleepy
2. Class C
3. When it's taken with nicotine
4. 24–30
5. Stimulants
6. 8 × 500 mg
7. Pain relief and the reduction of fever
8. They speed up reactions and make you more alert and awake
9. They slow down reactions and give you poor judgement of speed and distances
10. They suppress the pain sensors in the brain

Pages 30–31
1. Brain, liver and nervous system
2. One hour
3. Tar, nicotine and carbon monoxide
4. Emphysema, bronchitis, lung cancer and heart diseases
5. Cirrhosis
6. Carcinogens
7. They occur when people stop taking a drug when they are addicted
8. The carbon monoxide in tobacco deprives the foetus of oxygen
9. Carcinogens
10. When the body gets used to a drug so more and more of it is needed to have an effect

Pages 32–33
1. Virus, bacteria and fungi
2. Pathogens or germs
3. Mosquitoes carry malaria
4. They reproduce inside living cells and kill them
5. Athlete's foot and ringworm
6. To prevent the spread of infection
7. An organism that transports a disease from person to person, e.g. a mosquito
8. Skin, digestive, reproductive and respiratory systems and vectors
9. A virus
10. Food poisoning, tuberculosis, cholera

Pages 34–35
1. Penicillin
2. Phagocytes and lymphocytes
3. They engulf them
4. Antitoxins and antibodies
5. Because your body produces antibodies the first time you get it which remain in your body and fight the disease and destroy it before symptoms develop
6. They contain antigens on their surface

Pages 36–37
1. The brain
2. Antibodies are made to target specific antigens on pathogens
3. The lungs
4. The pancreas
5. The BCG
6. It deprives the foetus of oxygen and leads to a low birth weight
7. Nowhere, as it is extinct!
8. By using genetic engineering and bacteria to produce it in fermentation vessels
9. Malaria
10. Central nervous system consists of brain, spinal cord and nerve cells
11. Relay, sensory and motor
12. Diabetes
13. In the blood plasma
14. The flu virus changes regularly
15. HIV is a virus that has a high mutation rate
16. An organism that transports a pathogen from one organism to another, e.g. a mosquito
17. Phagocytes and lymphocytes
18. Natural immunity is when the body can remember a disease and produce antibodies to fight it before any symptoms develop
19. The body maintaining a constant internal environment
20. 140 years ago
21. Alleles
22. FSH, LH, oestrogen and progesterone
23. Bacteria
24. No, because measles is a virus: penicillin can only kill bacteria
25. Charles Darwin
26. Lamarck
27. There is a loss of energy in a food chain at each stage. Eventually there is not enough energy to support the next level of organism
28. Both, as a result of the predator/prey cycle
29. Organic farming
30. Inside the nucleus of your cells (except the red blood cells)

Pages 38–39
1 The nucleus
2 Elements are made of just one type of atom
3 By sharing electrons or by giving and taking electrons
4 O
5 Sodium
6 It consists of hydrogen atoms and oxygen atoms in the ratio two to one

Pages 40–41
1 In rows of seven
2 Sodium
3 Left no gaps
4 He left gaps, made predictions and swapped the order when he needed to
5 Properties
6 Increasing atomic number
7 Groups
8 1
9 3
10 Periods

Pages 42–43
1 Free electrons
2 Middle section
3 High melting point, high density, shiny, tough, hard-wearing, form coloured compounds and are good catalysts
4 Good electrical conductor which can be bent
5 Does not corrode or fracture
6 Iron is brittle
7 Bridges, buildings, ships, cars and trains
8 Haber process
9 It is very rare
10 It is too soft

Pages 44–45
1 Lithium, sodium and potassium
2 One
3 They have the same outer electron structure
4 Ionic
5 1+
6 Increases down the group
7 It is less dense than water
8 It burns with a squeaky pop
9 Sodium + water ➡ sodium hydroxide + water
10 Potassium + chlorine ➡ potassium chloride

Pages 46–47
1 Halogens
2 Decreases
3 Balloons and airships
4 It is less dense than air and it is not flammable
5 Electrical discharge tubes
6 Filament light bulbs
7 Lasers

Pages 48–49
1 Potassium chloride + water
2 Sodium sulphate + water
3 Carbon dioxide
4 Zinc chloride + water + carbon dioxide
5 Magnesium sulphate + water + carbon dioxide
6 Evaporate the water
7 Magnesium chloride + hydrogen
8 Zinc sulphate + hydrogen
9 Zinc chloride + water
10 Copper sulphate + water

Pages 50–51
1 Calcium carbonate
2 Sedimentary
3 Igneous
4 Neutralise acidity in lakes/soils
5 Calcium carbonate ➡ calcium oxide + carbon dioxide
6 Zinc carbonate ➡ zinc oxide + carbon dioxide
7 Sodium carbonate, carbon dioxide and water

Pages 52–53
1 Coal, oil and natural gas
2 Millions of years
3 Hydrogen and carbon
4 Runny, easy to ignite and have low boiling points
5 Short ones
6 At the top
7 They are more useful
8 Alkenes
9 A group of compounds with a similar number of carbon atoms

Pages 54–55
1 1 and 7
2 Seawater and underground deposits
3 Salt lowers the freezing point of water
4 Sodium chloride dissolved in water
5 Chlorine
6 Hydrogen
7 Sodium hydroxide
8 Bleach, purification of water, production of HCl and PVC
9 Manufacture of margarine
10 Soap, detergents, paper, rayon, acetate

Pages 56–57
1 Fruits, seeds and nuts
2 Seeds
3 Vitamins A and D
4 Fats can reach much higher temperatures than water
5 Fried
6 A chemical added to food that has passed safety tests and is approved for use throughout the European Union
7 To make the food look more attractive
8 To make layers mix together
9 To reduce the amount of sugar needed
10 No, arsenic is a natural substance which is highly toxic

Pages 58–59
1 C_2H_5OH
2 Drinks, solvents and as a fuel
3 They could become blind or even die
4 A purple dye and an unpleasant taste
5 Bio-diesel
6 Yeast
7 $C_6H_{12}O_6$
8 It becomes denatured
9 Phosphoric acid
10 Ethene + steam ➡ ethanol

Pages 60–61
1 20%
2 Nitrogen
3 Carbon dioxide, water vapour and noble gases
4 Carbon dioxide, steam, ammonia and methane
5 Carbon dioxide
6 The plants removed carbon dioxide and produced oxygen
7 It became locked up in sedimentary rocks and fossil fuels
8 Filters out harmful UV rays
9 New, more complex life forms could develop
10 Burning fossil fuels

Pages 62–63
1 Sulphur dioxide
2 Coal
3 If less electricity is needed then fewer fossil fuels will be burnt
4 It will have a yellow colour
5 Carbon dioxide
6 Carbon monoxide
7 Smoke particles
8 A reduction in the amount of sunlight that reaches the Earth's surface which may even affect weather patterns

Pages 64–65
1 Gold
2 They can be heated with carbon
3 Electrolysis
4 Haematite
5 Iron ore, coke and limestone
6 Oxygen from hot air
7 Carbon monoxide

Pages 66–67
1 Bauxite
2 It is soft and has a low density
3 An alloy
4 It is protected by a layer of aluminium oxide
5 Al_2O_3
6 Electrolysis
7 Oxide ions
8 Aluminium ions
9 Carbon, graphite
10 They react with oxygen to form carbon dioxide

Pages 68–69
1 When this gas is bubbled through limewater it turns the limewater cloudy
2 The gas bleaches damp litmus paper
3 The gas turns damp red litmus paper blue
4 Carbon dioxide
5 Lilac
6 Apple green
7 Orange

Pages 70–71
1 Carbon
2 Strength and stiffness
3 Stops body heat from escaping
4 Gloves and hats etc.
5 It is a thin membrane with many very small holes
6 Jackets and boots etc.
7 It is strong and lightweight

Pages 72–73
1 a) Limestone/marble/chalk
  b) Calcium oxide/carbon dioxide
  c) Ca(OH)$_2$
  d) Glass
2 a) Fractional distillation
  b) More flammable
  c) Cracking
3 C, A, D, B
4 a) Aluminium and titanium
  b) Aluminium
  c) Iron
  d) Copper
5 a) Nitrogen
  b) Carbon dioxide
  c) Venus and Mars
  d) Burning lots of fossil fuels
  e) Global warming/greenhouse effect
  f) Sulphur dioxide
6 a) Safety screen/goggles/gloves
  b) Sodium + water ➡ sodium hydroxide + hydrogen

Pages 74–75

1 Flow of charge
2 An ammeter
3 Several cells connected together
4 5 hours
5 Current which flows in just one direction
6 Changes light energy into electrical energy
7 A device which requires a low current, e.g. a calculator or instrument used in remote regions such as on the tops of mountains, in space, etc.

Pages 76–77

1 Ohms (Ω)
2 Dimmer switch
3 12 V
4 Light-dependent resistor (LDR), control street lighting
5 Thermistor, fire alarm

Pages 78–79

1 Alternating current
2 Stronger magnetic field, more coils
3 Acid rain/global warming

Pages 80–81

1 Mobile phones, fridges and freezers, televisions, radios, etc.
2 The telegraph
3 Mobile phones and the Internet
4 As a result of the need for such circuits in the space race
5 Many of them contain dangerous metal and so must be disposed of with great care

Pages 82–83

1 Once they have been used up they cannot be replaced
2 Sources of energy which can be replaced
3 Wood, wind, wave, sun, etc.
4 Hydroelectricity, tidal, wave

Pages 84–85

1 Electrical energy to motion (kinetic energy)
2 CD or DVD player, cassette player, electric drill, food mixer, hedge trimmer, electric lawn mower, fan, etc.
3 It rotates
4 Split ring commutator
5 Increase the current in the coil, increase the number of turns on the coil and increase the strength of the magnets
6 50%

Pages 86–87

1 A material which does not allow heat through it easily
2 Two panes of glass with air in between
3 Fibreglass in loft, double glazing, draft excluders, carpets and underlay, cavity wall insulation

4

Type of insulation	P/b time	Rank order
Double glazing	40 yrs	4
Cavity wall	10 yrs	3
Loft insulation	3 yrs	2
Draught excluders	4 yrs	1

5 The layer of air trapped between the curtain and the window is a good insulator and so reduces heat loss by conduction

Pages 88–89

1 a) 9 units
  b) 1 unit
  c) 3 units
  d) 2 units
  e) 1 unit
2 3 kW

Pages 90–91

1 a.c.
2 To protect the user and limit damage to equipment if a circuit is faulty
3 1 A, 3 A, 5A and 13 A
4 To protect a user should a circuit be faulty
5 Double insulation

Pages 92–93

1 Energy
2 25 waves produced by source each second
3 a) Light waves; b) sound waves
4 15 m/s
5 P-waves and S-waves
6 P-waves: longitudinal, faster, can travel through liquids
  S-waves: transverse, slower, cannot travel through liquids

Pages 94–95

1 They can travel through a vacuum, transverse
2 Wavelength and frequency
3 Radio, microwave, visible
4 Infrared, microwaves

Pages 96–97

1 No one knows the possible long-term effects of exposure to the microwaves used by the phones
2 Burning of the skin
3 Ultraviolet
4 Sunblock, clothing and staying out of the Sun
5 3000 m

Pages 98–99

1 It is totally internally reflected
2 As they travel they get weaker and so must be amplified
3 Unwanted distortions that are 'picked up' by a signal as it travels
4 Noise alters the shape of an analogue signal
5 The final signal received is a perfect copy of the original
6 New sounds have been created; music is distributed, stored and listened to in new ways

Pages 100–101

1 Gravitational forces
2 The orbit of a comet takes it very close and very far from the Sun: it is very elliptical
3 When they are closest to the Sun
4 A large rock which is likely to be orbiting the Sun between Mars and Jupiter
5 A near Earth object: a large NEO, such as an asteroid, could collide with Earth and destroy all life

Pages 102–103

1 The Milky Way
2 Gravitational forces
3 Nuclear fusion reactions
4 a) Black dwarf; b) supernova and black hole/neutron star
5 It continues to expand. It stops expanding and contracts, the Big Crunch. It may then explode and start to expand again

Pages 104–105

1 To avoid distortions caused by the Earth's atmosphere
2 Flyby probes do not land; an example of a flyby probe is Deep Space 1 and an example of a lander is Viking 2 Lander
3 They must take food, water and oxygen, and need a constant temperature, protection from radiation and enough fuel for return

Pages 106–107

1 Mercury, Mars and Pluto
2 Jupiter
3 Its temperature and atmosphere are closest to that of Earth
4 220 N
5 Smoke detectors, weather and communications satellites, space blankets, etc.

Pages 108–109

1 10 hours
2 Direct current
3 10 V
4 A resistor whose resistance decreases in bright light. Controlling street lighting
5 It led to the development of electrical circuits and components that were smaller, faster and more reliable than previous ones
6 Advantage: greater degree of freedom for the device using the batteries. Disadvantage: cost of electrical energy is higher and disposal of large numbers of batteries is a problem
7 Advantage: low technology therefore easy to use and maintain. Disadvantage: no wind, no electricity
8 Larger current, more turns on coil, stronger magnetic field
9 50%, lost to the surroundings (as heat)
10 a) Hot water jacket 2 years, loft insulation 5 years and double glazing 10 years; b) hot water jacket
11 6 units, 66 p
12 1200 W
13 The outer casing
14 Wind, tidal, solar, geothermal, etc.
15 100 m/s
16 a) A is gamma waves and B is radio waves; b) they can all be reflected, refracted and undergo diffraction. They all travel at the same speed in a vacuum; c) microwaves and infrared waves; d) ultraviolet waves and X-rays; e) X-rays
17 Waves which are emitted from the epicentre of an earthquake
18 Sun, planets, moons, asteroids and comets
19 Gravitational forces
20 The galaxy in which we live
21 An exploding star
22 The naked eye, telescopes, flyby probes, landers and manned flights
23 Exposure to radiation, weightlessness, maintaining a breathable air supply and survivable temperature range